Y0-BGD-044

A NEW HOLIDAY

TRAVEL GUIDE

ITALY

The New Holiday Guide to
ITALY

The New Holiday Travel Guide Series

M. Evans and Company   New York

Library of Congress Cataloging-in-Publication Data

The New Holiday guide to Italy.

  (The New holiday travel guide series;)
  Includes index.
  1. Italy—Description and travel—1975-   —Guidebooks. I. Series.
DG416.N47   1988   914.5′04928   87-5436

ISBN 0-87131-507-6

Copyright © 1960, 1962, 1964, 1966, 1968, 1971, 1973, 1976,
1979, 1982, 1988 by RD Publications, Inc. All rights reserved
under International and Pan-American Copyright Conventions.

ISBN: 0-87131-507-6
Manufactured in the United States of America
1 2 4 6 8 9 7 5 3
Revised First Edition

General Editor: Theodore Fischer

M. Evans and Company, Inc.
216 East 49 Street
New York, New York 10017

CONTENTS

CHAPTER *1*

ITALY: THE LAND AND ITS PEOPLE

Italy is a land of antique beauty, and while you are there the past will be always with you. But what is likely to impress you most about Italy today is its endless variety: The glaciers of the Dolomites and the temples of Agrigento, the barren hills of Calabria and the asphodel meadows of Tuscany, the water-borne beauty of Venice and the cliffside grandeur of Taormina.

We think of Italy as the heir of Rome, an ancient country; but geologically Italy is very young. It is important to remember this, for the circumstances of its formation have been significant in all of its history. Formed in the depth of the sea, the Italian peninsula was thrust up, sank again, rose once more. Later, along one side, a chunk of primordial mountain plunged again into the sea.

It was this prolonged creation that gave Italy its contours, its plains and mountains, its variety of soils and climates. When you have seen Italy, you may be tempted to believe that its history was made by its geography. In a sense, you will be right. Despite its rugged mountain ranges, Italy always has been primarily agricultural. The fertile zones of the peninsula—the plains of primitive Latium and Campania Felix, where its history began—were created by vast volcanic eruptions that mantled the rocky fragments of the mountains and smoothed out the coast line. The early inhabitants, protected from the ocean and provided with a fertile land, were men of the soil—earthsprung peasants and tillers, builders and soldiers.

Centuries before Rome or the long duel with Carthage or the conquest of the Mediterranean, Italy had been started on the path of imperial expansion by her geographical heritage.

Geography also colored the development of the country from the days of the warring tribes to the present modern republic. Split by mountain ranges, segmented into self-contained little areas and shut off from their neighbors, separated by vast differences in climate and terrain, Italy has been politically and culturally divided. For centuries the "natural" units of Italy were small geographical regions—in some cases, even the cities within them. To this day, each unit preserves its own distinctive air, traditions, customs and outlook on life.

As you move about Italy, you see how little time has done to obliterate their ancient differences; often it seems to have sharpened them into regional characteristics. The Neapolitan has a reputation for exuberance, gaiety and sentimentality; the Sicilian for pride, clannishness and a burning loyalty. The Genoese is noted for his rough-hewn directness and business acumen; the Florentine for his intellectual refinement, artistry, tendency to argue and extraordinary use of profanity. The Venetian is easy-going, somewhat subtle, skeptical and cynical; the Umbrian, simple and devout; the Sardinian aloof, tenacious and reserved.

Although these are stereotypes, over-simplifications—even distortions—there is a grain of psychological truth in them and they at least illuminate the astonishing diversity of the country.

The cities of Italy vary no less than its people. In what other country will you find cities as startlingly unlike as Florence and Venice, Milan and Naples, Bologna and Palermo, Verona and Cagliari? And the differences are not simply in location and climate and language, but the product of a long history, a reflection of the time when each was a fiercely autonomous city-state with its own political and social structure, its own diplomacy, its own dreams of military and financial expansion.

National unity (a concept that implied the elevation of one city or region to a position of dominance as the capital and seat of government) was slow to take root in individualistic Italy. The city-states preferred the political maneuvering which preserved a precarious balance of power throughout the peninsula, the sly art which Lorenzo de' Medici practiced with such consummate skill toward the end of the 15th century.

Columns of the Temple of Juno at Agrigento

Hydrofoils leaving Naples for Capri and Ischia

No country is all of a piece, single and unified. But in Italy there is no end to variety and contrast. Yet through it all runs the unifying thread of tradition. In the Sardinian peasant's house, the shape of the flour bin is the same as his ancestor's in Roman times. So is the beaked jar on the table, the vat molded like an amphor, the trinkets and amulets. The Lucanian farmer separates chaff from wheat by the same method and on the same kind of threshing floor which his forebears used, and in the fields his oxen are yoked precisely as they might have been 2000 years ago. Even the peasants' houses have a characteristic style in each region, and in many villages the home built yesterday is a duplicate of those that have been standing for centuries.

In this country of the ancient past, history is a living presence that has survived in the life and customs of the people. Today's Italians are modern, as avid as any for the latest products of science and technology. But behind them stretches the guiding tradition of a history that makes them peculiarly the heirs of the past. But the persistence of the past into the present also has its divisive aspects. It emphasizes the shocking contrasts which for generations have scarred the country. Italy seems almost to have two civilizations, to live in two eras simultaneously.

Culturally, modern Italy stands among the most advanced countries in the world. Her achievements in the post-war period have been especially striking: Her physicists, chemists and mathematicians have made basic contributions to modern science. Literature, art, architecture, music, all have had a new renaissance. Students from all over the world flock to Italian universities.

But beside and beneath this brilliant learning exists an Italy of medieval backwardness and superstition. The Apulian farmer still believes that goblins come at night to braid the manes and tails of his horses, still inclines to the magic-healer rather than to the doctor when his child is sick. In Sardinia, a young man refrains from giving his bride combs or a pair of scissors, lest she become sharp-tongued or fall under the spell of a sorceress. And his mother-in-law carefully pours a glass of water over the threshold of the nuptial room to thwart the evil spirits.

Such contrasts are, to some extent, common to all countries; but in the more primitive parts of Italy they work themselves into the whole pattern of life.

Primitive and modern, scholarly and illiterate, urbane and childlike —the cleavage exists everywhere. Northern Italy is up-to-date, industrial, alert to the uses of invention and advanced in scientific techniques. The region in the triangle of Genoa, Turin and Bologna produces 80 per cent of Italy's manufactured goods. Factories are well-equipped, cities impressively modern, people enterprising and prosperous.

But the South has traditionally been an impoverished land—dry, eroded, scarred by centuries of social inequality and neglect. In the most remote and backward districts—in Basilicata and Calabria— there was, until lately, almost no industry and little business activity. Here feudalism continued into the 20th century, with absentee ownership of land, concentration of property in the hands of a few, little contact with the rest of the country—and the continual flight of the ablest people from poverty and despair. For generations, all these combined to drive the "other" Italy still further from the North, still deeper into social and economic stagnation.

But today in the South the effects of a slow transformation can be seen. The malarial swamps of the lowlands have been reclaimed, and irrigation provided for arid regions. Drinking water has been piped into towns that were without it. Large estates have been broken up into small holdings and distributed to peasants. Capital is being provided for industrial development. Illiteracy and superstition are giving way to education; health services have been provided; whole new villages have been established in depressed areas. Out of the catastrophe of World War II came a rebirth of social awareness and a commitment to development of the South, an effort which continues today.

The Italian has lost none of his old interest in politics. The spectrum of parties runs all the way from extreme conservatism through Christian Democracy, liberalism, republicanism, socialistic democracy and socialism, to communism. To the Italians, such political fragmentation is the faithful reflection of the natural diversity of opinion and at the same time a guarantee against the domination of any single party. It is thus a protection against the creation of a totalitarian regime, an experience of government that the Italians of today have no intention of repeating.

Monastery of San Damiano, Assisi   *The view from Taormina*

Italy today is still the classic land of history and beauty and art. Italy is Rome and Caesar and the Imperial Legions on the Appian Way. It is the moment of time preserved at Pompeii and the beauty fixed forever in the temples at Agrigento. It is St. Peter's and the Sistine Chapel, Michelangelo and Botticelli, Galileo and Dante, Venice and Syracuse.

But it is more than a window on history, a museum of antiquities. Italy is vital, alive in the present, and in the mood and temper of its people is the key to today's Italy. The Italian character is the unifying element of the diversity, the complexity of this country of contrasts.

Like his country, the Italian seems to be a study in contradictions. Temperamental and vibrant, he is at the same time firmly realistic. He may be susceptible to tawdry eloquence, but he is prone to second thoughts that are liberally seasoned with skepticism. He is proud of the glorious past, but painfully aware of present shortcomings and failures. A practical man with an inquisitive interest in scientific matters, he refuses to submit to the machinery he loves to handle. Deeply Christian in his concept of the individual soul and the dignity of man, he often is captivated by colorful formality. He is positive to the point of stubbornness, but he understands tolerance and is inclined to compromise differences.

And beneath this militant individualism are the deep bonds which hold together the people and the country: Consciousness of his history, a sharing of the golden glory that was Rome, a common religion, a fierce pride in great art and literature, a will to rebuild from disaster a world of freedom and equality.

And above all there is the passionate love of life and beauty that always has been the special mark of Italy.

CHAPTER 2

ITALY: THE BACKGROUND

There are keys to Italy.

Traveling through the country, you cannot fail to see that Italy is the past extended into the present, the heir of 4000 years of visible history and in many ways parent of all the Western world. At the same time, Italy is among the youngest of modern states—a nation of 57 million people which, after centuries of turmoil and decades of political repression, has recently taken its place among the democratic powers.

Finally, you should remember that although these people are Italians to the world, at home and at heart they remain Romans, Sicilians, Neapolitans and Florentines.

Italy is a modern, flourishing nation. But perhaps more than any other people today, the Italians are the product of their past. They are aware of it and proud of it, united and divided by it.

The history of Italy begins with many legends and few facts. Nearly every schoolboy knows the story of Romulus and Remus and the wolf that suckled them. There are the seven hills and the tale of the Sabine women and the Tarpeian Rock at the edge of the Capitoline from which criminals and those who offended the gods were flung to their death.

The historic beginnings are vague. We know that there were people in Italy 4000 years ago, but not who they were or where they came from. About the 8th century B.C. the pattern becomes clear. At that time there were three major groups in what is now Italy. The northern border was occupied by Gauls and other European peoples who had probably trickled down from the Danube Basin in Central Europe. The area from the Tiber north to the Po was held by the Etruscans. The southern end of the Peninsula, including Sicily, was Greek. These three groups, with the native Italian tribes, were the beginnings of the Italy you will see today.

Palazzo Pubblico, landmark of Siena

The Etruscans, perhaps the most important historically, and certainly the most intriguing, appeared in Italy about 800 B.C., and though the countryside is littered with the remains of their civilization, we still know very little about their origins. Herodotus, the Greek historian, identified them as a people from Asia Minor. His evidence was doubted for many years, but modern scholars now are inclined to accept his opinion.

For one thing, the Etruscan language was unrelated to any European tongue. Hundreds of inscriptions—written in a deceptively simple variation of the Greek alphabet—remain, but nobody has yet succeeded in finding a key to them. We do know that the Etruscan civilization was the mold from which Rome was made. Artisans and craftsmen, architects and agriculturalists, workers in iron and bronze, skilled goldsmiths and potters, they planted the seeds from which grew the world's greatest empire.

You will see collections of Etruscan art in many museums—in Florence, which has the greatest; in Rome, in Tarquinia, even in Sicily. You can see the remarkable tomb paintings and sarcophagi in the necropolis at Cerveteri, at Tarquinia, at Veio and at Volterra. They were a great and creative people, these Etruscans, and what grew from their stock was even greater.

The Greek civilization that flourished in the south was no less important and the remains are even more impressive. From the 7th to the 3rd century B.C., there was a great flowering of Hellenic culture and wherever you go you may see the solid remnants of it: The Temple of Neptune at Paestum just south of Naples; the great 5th century B.C. theaters in Syracuse and Taormina in Sicily; the magnificent temples on the acropolis at Agrigento (Concordia is thought by many to be the best preserved of all Greek temples), and at Segesta and Selinunte. Messina and Catania were among the richest and most powerful of the Greek colonies, and for centuries Syracuse was second only to Athens in importance. Pindar and Aeschylus lived there, Plato visited the city a number of times, and Archimedes was killed there while directing its defense.

There were civilizations to the north and to the south, but it was in the central plains around Rome that the story unfolded. After the seven legendary kings, the Roman tribes formed what was called a republic, at the end of the 6th century B.C. It was aristocratic, patrician and limited, but at least it did represent the will of a group rather than of one leader.

Under the Republic, the conquest of the world began—first the neighboring tribes, then the Etruscans, then the Greeks to the south. The struggle lasted for centuries. Pyrrhus, greatest of the generals from Greece, was called in to halt the Roman expansion. He won every battle, but his "Pyrrhic victories" left Rome the master of the whole peninsula.

Once they were in control, the Romans literally paved the way to empire with a network of roads that were not equaled until a hundred years ago. Parts of those built before the birth of Christ still survive; and to this day, as you drive through Italy, you will see the ancient markers that record the distance to Rome.

Expansion brought conflict, and powerful Carthage stood in the way, first in Sicily and then across the Mediterranean in Africa. The Punic Wars were a matter of another century, for Hamilcar and after him Hannibal and Hasdrubal were formidable opponents. When Hannibal bore down from the Alps with his elephant tanks, Rome was close to collapse. But when the 3rd Punic War ended in 146 B.C., Rome was master of Spain and the Mediterranean islands; and Carthage itself had been razed, its site plowed and sown with salt.

Conquest brought the desire for more conquest. Philip II of Macedonia was defeated. Greece went down and with her the Achaean League. Egypt became a vassal. Rome was master of all the Mediterranean world west of India.

But with success came trouble at home—corruption and the abuse of power, slave revolts that were put down with unspeakable barbarity. Out of it all came reform, the First Triumvirate of 60 B.C., with Pompey the popular hero; Crassus, who furnished unlimited funds for soldiers and circuses; and Caesar, young, capable and ambitious. It took ten years of hard campaigning in Gaul to make Caesar master of Rome. He crossed the Rubicon (near Rimini) in 49 B.C., and five years later lay dead of dagger wounds. He had destroyed the Republic and founded the Empire.

The Republic had lasted about four centuries, the Empire another five. And this 900 years is only a fraction of what lies before you.

Caesar was succeeded by another triumvirate—his grandnephew and adopted son, Octavian; Marc Antony; and Lepidus. In the 2nd Triumvirate it was Octavian who survived; in turn he became *princeps* (leader), *imperator* (commander) and, as Augustus, emperor. He was the first and perhaps the greatest of them all. Two things of supreme importance happened before he died in 14 A.D.: The Empire reached its greatest extent, from Mesopotamia to England; and in Bethlehem was born a child who was to found an empire far greater than Augustus ever dreamed about.

Augustus was a wise and creative ruler whose reign ushered in two centuries of a golden age of peace throughout the world. But at home he was followed by rulers whose names, with one or two exceptions, have become synonymous with evil: Tiberius, a paranoid who suspected many and murdered all he suspected; Caligula, a sadistic madman who delighted in colossal orgies that inevitably ended in death for the participants; Claudius, a timid, stuttering man who murdered in fear and self-defense but withal an able administrator; and Nero, the pyromaniac whose specialty was the persecution of Christians.

What you see today are fragments of the city that have survived 2000 years of destruction at the hands of nature and man. Rome in those days was the wonder of the world, a metropolis of close to one and a half million people crowded within the Aurelian Walls, in half the space occupied by the modern city. Three-, four- and five-story apartments crowded narrow streets, and profiteering landlords threw up more jerry-built warrens on every available space. The tenants climbed to the upper stories by ladders, smoke from braziers poured out of the unglazed windows, and household slops were cast out to run sluggishly in the gutters of the alleys.

The rich occupied the lower floors and the poor climbed higher, but nobody stayed at home very much. All were out early to the baths or to the street barbers for the news, the day's work was customarily finished by noon or shortly after, and the rest of the day was spent in pleasure and amusement. A good part of the population was only casually occupied with their duties for the rich patrons who were obliged to support them, and there were times when as many as two or three hundred thousand unemployed lived at public expense—the *Annona* who received free corn from the state. All day long the streets were crowded with loungers and beggars and streethawkers and merchants and porters, and more than half the days of the year were holidays.

The great distractions provided for a half-idle populace by emperors and men of wealth and ambition were the games. In the early days, they were day-long athletic competitions; but as one benefactor after another attempted to endear himself to the masses, the games were extended to three days, a week, a month and even longer. However meager life at home might be, there were always, even for the slaves, the sybaritic pleasures of the public baths and the excitement of the circus.

The great spectacles were held in the Colosseum. Tickets were distributed the night before the show and by the time the performance began, the amphitheater was jammed to its 50,000-capacity. The day-long performance began quietly with wild animals loosed in the arena to tear each other to bits—a sport so popular that in time the empire was denuded of bears and elephants and tigers. Then men were brought in to fight the animals with snares and knives and nets; and, as the day wore on, the gladiators appeared to fight to death while commoner and slave and emperor and Vestal Virgins screamed for blood—"Jugula! Jugula!" (Slit his throat!)

It was a costly show. Sometimes it was necessary to use criminals to slaughter each other, or Christians who were fed to ravenous animals. And sometimes, as a special treat, a netful of naked women was suspended just within reach of the beasts. Nero invented a new amusement: He crucified Christians upside down, covered them with pitch, and then set them on fire. The Apostle Peter probably suffered that fate.

Roman theater in Tuscolo, near Frascati

This was Rome, the heart of the Empire and the center of the world. The great days of conquest were past and the Roman Empire was about to come to an end.

There were moments of reprieve. Trajan made new conquests in Asia. Hadrian built his great wall across the north of England to hold back the encroaching tribes of Picts. The philosopher Marcus Aurelius wrote his famous *Meditations* while he continued the persecutions of the Christians. Diocletian made an effort to pull the Empire together once more, but Constantine, who followed him, moved the capital to ancient Byzantium, divided the Empire and, by his conversion to Christianity, made way for the new era. The barbarians swept down the peninsula again and again, and when, 150 years later in 476, the Teutonic chief Odoacer became emperor, the Roman Empire became history.

Rome fell to the barbarians, we say. And in the sense that the conquerors were not Italian, that is true. But they were not hairy savages dressed in skins. They were the people who for generations had been doing the work of Rome on the frontiers. When Rome died at the center, they took over. Theodoric, for example, made a respectable effort to restore the Empire to its former glory. He reestablished the Church of Rome and secured many of the old boundaries. But new waves of attackers swept down from Europe and the remnants of Rome were at last buried beneath them.

The centuries between the fall of Rome and the beginning of the Renaissance were as dark in Italy as they were elsewhere in Europe. The Church, besieged by military leaders and beset by internal divisions and dissensions, managed to keep alive the spirit of Christianity and the respect for learning. In the darkest days of the Middle Ages, the Moorish invaders in Spain preserved the knowledge of the East and, in their great centers of learning, became the instructors to Europe and to all the world.

But cruel and benighted as they were, the Middle Ages were not without purpose, for out of them and out of the pockets of learning which they sheltered grew the Renaissance which opened the modern era. It was in Italy that this great wave, this deluge of art and creativity, burst upon the world at the end of the 14th century.

The Church was one factor in the revival and rebirth of art and learning. But there were others. There was the growth during the Middle Ages of the power and importance of the city-states—Milan, Pisa, Venice, Florence, Naples—jealous, warring municipalities that often were under the control of one of the feudal families. In Milan it was the Sforzas; in Ferrara, the Este family; in Florence, the famous Medici. Rich, lavish, learned, and often unspeakably evil, these families and their open-handed patronage of the arts contributed to the resurrection of learning.

The Florence of the Medici cradled the Renaissance. Perhaps it was the heritage of Etruscan creativity, the generous support of patrons or the extraordinary crafts and skills that had been nurtured and developed by the guilds of artisans. The incredible fact is that in this one small city there appeared within a century or so the greatest array of genius the world has ever known. It was there that Dante set the character of Italian literature with his *Divine Comedy,* and Boccaccio, following him, wrote the *Decameron.* In art, Cimabue and Giotto laid the foundations of the Renaissance. After them came the greatest names in the history of art: Fra Angelico, Verrocchio, Leonardo da Vinci, Michelangelo, Donatello, Botticelli, Ghiberti, Cellini and a dozen others.

And Florence produced more than artists. Galileo perfected the telescope here and made his first observations of the planets; Savonarola preached his fiery sermons and was hanged and burned; and Machiavelli founded the modern science of politics with his treatise, *The Prince.*

The Renaissance flowed outward from Florence to Pisa, to Ravenna, to Venice, to Rome, and at last to the whole world. It ended the Middle Ages and began the modern era.

By the 18th century, Italy had become little more than a pawn in the European game of politics. Split into weak and divided states, it became in turn the victim of Spanish, Austrian and French ambitions. The Hapsburgs bled the country; Napoleon ravished and robbed it. It was not until the middle of the 19th century that the idea of national unity took hold. It was begun by a young Genoese lawyer named Mazzini and later was supported by the legendary Giuseppe Garibaldi. Both were forced to leave the country, but the revolutionary elements which they had created were welded by a Piedmontese nobleman, Count Camillo Benso di Cavour. When Garibaldi returned from exile in 1860, his army of "red shirts" tipped the scales and in 1861 Victor Emmanuel was crowned king of a united Italy. In 1870 Rome became the capital.

Mussolini and his black shirts took over Italy in 1922, and attempted, perhaps, to recreate Imperial Rome. This Fascist government managed to make the trains run on time (they still do) and instituted sanitation and other reforms. Unfortunately, Mussolini also created a much feared and hated secret police. He led Italy into World War II as a subservient ally of Germany. When Italy was knocked out of the war, it became a fierce battleground for Allied and Nazi armies. The Italians endured hunger, bombings, and fear. In 1945, Mussolini, a pompous dictator, was caught by Italian partisans and shot, then hanged in Milan.

The next year the Italian voters made Italy a republic. The big task was rebuilding the cities and the economy. And the feat has been accomplished—in the first years, the American Marshall Plan helped; since then Italian industry has blossomed. There have also been setbacks. In 1966, floods damaged or destroyed many of Florence's art treasures. As a result Italians are more aware of conserving their natural and cultural resources. But exactly how, is still a question.

Italy is periodically plagued by earthquakes. One of the worst in recent years occurred in November, 1980. It caused widespread damage in the provinces of Salerno, Benevento and Avellino in the region of Basilicata, and in the Potenza province of Campania, even extending to Naples. One hundred twenty-six towns were severely damaged, although fortunately they were not in heavily populated areas.

Strikes are an ever-present accompaniment of social change in Italy, and government bureaucracy is a rather sad joke. In an effort to increase government efficiency, in 1972, regions were given more autonomy while, in the area of civil rights, long-standing pressure resulted in liberalized divorce, birth control and abortion legislation. The Christian Democrat Party, Italy's leading party, has been forced to share its governing role with the smaller parties, especially the Socialist Party. The influence of the second-largest party in Italy, the Communist Party has been waning in the 1980's and in particular after the death in 1984 of its charismatic leader Enrico Berlinguer.

As for the economic picture, the country is fighting unemployment, particularly among young people. Inflation figures, however, are dropping, and at present the annual inflation rate is at about 6 percent.

CHAPTER 3

WHAT YOU SHOULD KNOW ABOUT ITALY

It is said that the Italian welcome is as warming and exhilarating as a glass of fine wine. The reason Italians are such good hosts is that they get so much practice—Italy may be the most popular country in Europe. Travelers find the sun right for sunbathing year round, and viewing the Sistine Chapel and Italy's other art treasures is always in season.

PLANNING YOUR TRIP

Passport and Medical Requirements. All an American citizen needs to enter Italy is a valid passport, obtainable from the U.S. Passport Agency, which has offices in New York, Chicago, Boston, Washington, D.C., San Francisco, New Orleans, Detroit, Los Angeles, Houston, Philadelphia, Seattle, Stamford, Honolulu and Miami. In many towns, the local courthouse or post office will have forms. You must apply in person, bringing with you a proof of citizenship (birth or baptismal certificate), two recent photographs 2½ inches square, and $35 for a ten-year non-renewable passport. Your passport will be mailed to you anywhere from three days to six weeks after, so it is best to apply well in advance of your departure.

Vaccination is no longer required.

No visa is needed unless you plan to stay more than 90 days.

Getting Information. The Italian Government Travel Office will send you reams of reliable data and advice, including photos, all gratis. Write or visit their offices: 630 Fifth Avenue, New York, NY 10111, 212-245-4822; 500 N. Michigan Avenue, Chicago, IL 60611, 312-644-0990; 360 Post Street, San Francisco, CA 94108, 415-392-5266; 3 Place Ville Marie, Montreal, Quebec H3B 2E3, 514-866-7667.

Many ages at a glance—the Forum of Trajan and the Nome di Maria Church in Rome.

Travel Agents. You may want a travel agent's help if you are planning to see a large number of places in a short time; if you are traveling in peak periods and are not on a tight budget; if you want all arrangements made in advance. The international airlines also offer packages and will book hotels for you with no charge.

As a rule, travel agents do not charge for booking plane or boat reservations, but do charge for their services if you ask them to plan your tour and make the arrangements. Their fee is usually paid by the supplier (airline, hotel, car rental firm, etc.) in the form of a percentage commission on your expenditures.

Air Transportation: TWA and Pan offer nonstop service from New York to Rome and Milan with connections to other U.S. cities. Alitalia, the Italian flag-carrier, flies to Rome and Milan from New York, Boston, Chicago, Toronto, and Montreal. CP Air has nonstops Toronto/Montreal-Rome, and Montreal-Milan. Most European airlines offer connecting service between major North American cities and Rome and Milan.

WEATHER—AND WHEN TO GO

Italy is a comparatively small country and an exceedingly popular one with tourists. The result is that during the summer months, the hotels, the restaurants, the sights of notable interest, the trains, buses, and highways are extremely crowded. If you can possibly manage to make your trip to Italy in the spring or fall, you will fare much better —not only because spring and fall are beautiful seasons in Italy, but because you will find accommodations much more easily, and in some cases they will cost you considerably less out of season.

Important point: if you would like to do a good deal of shopping in Italy, don't plan your trip for August. The 15th of August, called *Ferragosto,* is the beginning of the official Italian holiday season, when the majority of offices and stores close, some of them for only a day or

Castelle d'Ischia, built in 1441

two, re-opening a few days after the holiday with a skeleton staff, others to remain closed for the rest of the month. August, then, is not the time to plan on having a silk dress made to order in Rome or Florence. All shopping goes into a general slump, for the selection in the stores that *are* open tends to be meager.

Weather is not a problem in Italy, for to a greater extent than in most countries you can choose what you like. There is considerable variation from north to south; from mountainous regions to level plains; and from seaside localities to inland ones. In general, the climate is temperate. In the Dolomites and Italian Alps, summer weather is cool, bright, and sunny, frequently cold at night. There is snow in most of the mountain resorts through March and frequently later, depending on the altitude. Milan is cool and sometimes foggy in early spring and late fall, while it ranges from moderate to hot in summer. Venice can be raw and cold in late fall and early spring, varies from moderate to hot and sticky in summer. It is at its best in late spring and early fall. Florence can be downright hot in summer, surrounded as it is by hills which cut off the cooling breezes. Rome also can be hot in summer, but nearly always toward evening a sea breeze, called the *Ponentino,* springs up, and for outdoor dining a light wrap is frequently advisable. Spring and fall are the best times for Sicily.

WHAT YOU SHOULD TAKE

Most well-known medicines and many American brands of cosmetics and various toiletries, cleansing tissues, and other near-necessities are available throughout Italy. There is no necessity to travel with oddments enough to stock a small drugstore. But do remember to bring a soap dish and soap, since most hotels still do not supply soap in the bathroom.

As for clothes, that depends largely on where you're going and what you're planning to do. Italians are extremely fashion-conscious. They probably give more thought to their clothes than Americans whether they are heading for the beach or meeting someone for an appointment in the city. For visiting cities such as Rome, Florence, or Milan, a lightweight suit is advisable for a man in summer; for fashionable restaurants and nightclubs, a dark blue or gray suit. In winter, a dinner jacket is essential for opening nights at the opera; otherwise a dark blue or gray suit can be worn anywhere. For women, comfortable sight-seeing shoes are a must—but a pair of dressier shoes for dining out are nearly as essential since Italian women are very dressy indeed. In many churches, sleeveless or backless dresses are frowned upon, so even on a hot day a light jacket is a handy if you plan to visit churches. In summer (except in the mountains), a raincoat is probably all the top-coat you're likely to need, if you have a sweater, jacket, or shawl to put on for dining outdoors, or attending outdoor performances at night. But in spring and fall a topcoat *is* essential.

CUSTOMS REGULATIONS

Tourists entering Italy need not pay duty on personal effects such as 2 still cameras (plus 10 rolls of film), one movie camera (plus 10 rolls of film) or items for their own use. This includes not more than 20 packs of cigarettes (400 cigarettes) or 500 grams of smoking tobacco or cigars. You do need a special permit to bring in a gun. If you bring in a portable radio (or have a radio in your car), you may have to pay a radio tax for the period you remain in Italy. But you are allowed two bottles of wine and one of liquor per person, if you are so minded.

Leaving Italy, you may not take out more than 5,000,000 lire in lire banknotes, and you can't take out more dollars than the amount brought in. This means you should retain receipts when you change money, so that you can easily reconvert your currency before leaving Italy. Art objects, paintings, and sculpture, may not be taken or sent out of Italy without a certificate from the Fine Arts section of the Ministry of Public Instruction. Most dealers and gallery owners will make arrangements to have this done for you.

United States residents may bring back with them, duty free, purchases amounting to $400 per person. The articles must be acquired as an incident of the trip and be intended for the visitor's personal or household use. Gifts not exceeding $50 in value may be sent to persons in the United States free of duty.

While you are abroad, you may have purchases shipped to your address in the United States. For some reason, travelers often burden themselves unnecessarily with bulky and inconvenient parcels which they have collected. That's unnecessary. You can mail the little ones, and American Express will relieve you of the big ones.

To simplify proceedings when you land in the United States, it's a good idea to keep the sales slips for your purchases all together for reference when you fill out your declaration and, if necessary, to show the customs officer. In Italy sales slips are now customarily given with all purchases. You can also request an invoice, for which you may have to pay the tax stamp (500 lire). The storekeeper may ask you to come by for it a few days later since he will have to compute ad valorum taxes. But if the purchase is sizable and it would be difficult for you to return a second time, it is permissible to insist that it be done immediately. Try to avoid handwritten receipts, which do not show tax. In Italy the customer is obliged to have receipts on leaving a shop. This is also true of restaurants, so don't leave your "bill" on the table: It's actually your receipt.

Visitors to Italy are expected to register with the police within three days of their arrival to get a *permesso di soggiorno* (permission for a stay). It's a centuries-old system which unfortunately still survives. When you stop at a hotel, you merely leave your passport at the desk and the matter is taken care of. But if you stay with friends for any length of time, you or your host must go to the central police station. (In Rome, 15 Via San Vitale.)

GETTING AROUND IN ITALY

By car. The best way to see the country is probably by car—if you are not afraid of coping with Italian drivers. The new road-safety code has tamed them somewhat—but only somewhat. Chief points for the unwary American motorist to bear in mind are that the car coming from the right has the right of way; that horn-blowing is illegal in cities, but required at curves and intersections in the country during daylight hours. Parking lights are used for city driving at night with brighter lights flashed at intersections or as a passing signal.

If you bring your own car into Italy, you should remember that gas, which is sold by the liter, is very expensive. One liter is approximately equivalent to one quart. Also, if your car is a big one, it may be not only expensive but complicated to drive. Italian roads were not designed for large cars; many city streets are altogether too narrow for them, and parking places are difficult to find. Now that European small cars have become so popular in the United States, many Americans take advantage of the opportunity to buy one in Europe at a substantial saving over the American price. Any foreign-car dealer will tell you how to go about getting delivery of your car in Italy at the time you want it.

For most people, renting a car in Italy is the most practical solution. Car rental firms, including the familiar Hertz (Via Sallustiana 28; Tel. 46.33.36 in Rome), are to be found in all large cities. Travel agencies can furnish you with a list of other reputable firms, and they are also, of course, listed in the telephone directory under *Autonoleggi*. Members of the American Automobile Association can make arrangements to rent a car before leaving the United States. A deposit, which is refunded when the car is returned, is usually required. Rates range from $30–$40 dollars a day, plus about 30 cents a kilometer, for the most popular small Italian cars. Gas costs the equivalent of about $3.40 per gallon. Insurance usually amounts to an extra $9 and the person renting the car pays for the gas and oil. With many firms you can rent a car in one city and leave it in another; there is no additional charge for this service.

Road maps are available at major gas stations. Particularly detailed maps, guidebooks, and tourist information are available from the Touring Club of Italy (7/A Via Ovidio in Rome, Tel. 38.86.58; and 10 Corso Italia in Milan, Tel. 8526).

By train. Italy is served by an extensive network of trains with accommodations in two classes, first and second. Most trains carry both classes but some de luxe expresses are first class only. The various types of services are always indicated, but the descriptive word used is somewhat less than accurate. Trains range in excellence from *rapido* (fast express, with surcharge of 40 per cent over the ticket price) to *direttissimo* (express with a few stops), *diretto* (more stops), and *locale* (slow local). On many of the fast express trains, seat reservations are obligatory; in other cases they are advisable. Reservations on a *rapido* cost 2,200 lire extra.

The price of a train ticket depends on the distance you are traveling and the class; there is a round-trip reduction usually only on trips of less than 250 kilometers. Normal price for a 500-kilometer trip (315 miles), for example, is 43,800 lire (about $32) in first class, 24,300 lire (about $17.35) in second.

Sleeping-car reservations may be obtained only through Wagon Lits, or through your hotel *portiere* (concierge) or a travel agency who will book them through Wagon Lits for you. You can also buy a sleeping-car ticket at the railroad station but it should be done at least three days in advance. These sleeping cars are part of the Italian Railway system and are known as "cuscette."

Eurailpass is a railroad pass which may be bought in the United States and which allows the owner, in whose name it is issued, a period of unrestricted travel, first class, on trains in fifteen countries—Austria, Belgium, Denmark, Finland, France, Germany, Greece, Holland, Italy, Luxembourg, Norway, Portugal, Spain, Sweden, and Switzerland. It costs $350 for 21 days, $440 for a month, $620 for two months, $760 for three months (children 4–12, half price; under 4, free). The ticket can also be bought in Italy (at Termini Station in Rome).

By plane. Italy is served by airlines of many nations, including the Italian *Alitalia,* for flights within the country, as well as abroad. For trips between Italy and other countries, extensive schedules are maintained by most of the major European lines, as well as TWA and Pan American. All of them maintain ticket offices in Rome and many of them in other cities as well. Travel agents anywhere can arrange reservations for you.

By inter-city bus. Bus travel is steadily gaining in popularity among tourists in Italy, and with good reason. The buses in use today are swift, modern and remarkably comfortable. Most of them are equipped with an English-speaking hostess, and the more luxurious ones boast washrooms, radio, and bar service. Routes are carefully planned for sightseeing pleasure. CIT, at the central railway station and at 64 Piazza della Republica in Rome and with branches in all large cities, has many excellent tours. Seat reservations must be made ahead of time. Thirty kilos (sixty-six pounds) of luggage per person are carried free. CIT also offers scheduled service between major cities, as well as to some smaller ones of interest such as Siena and Amalfi. Tickets cost roughly 100 lire per kilometer. Thus a ticket for a trip to Venice from Rome would cost about 57,000 lire ($40).

The Hermitage of Carceri in Umbria

By taxi. In Italy taxis do not cruise, but wait for passengers at cab stands, marked by yellow lines on the pavement at various spots throughout the city. If you don't find a taxi stand nearby, you can phone for one yourself or ask someone to call for you by dialing 3570.

A list of the standard charges is posted in each cab. Be sure the driver pulls down his flag as you start (it will already be down when he arrives, if you have telephoned for a cab, since you pay mileage from the stand), so that there can be no argument about the fare. In Rome rates are 2,800 lire for the first 200 meters or one minute, and 200 lire for each additional 300 meters or one minute. There is an additional charge of 500 lire for a trunk. Between 10:00 P.M. and 7:00 A.M. there is also an extra charge of 2,500 lire. You also pay 1,000 lire extra on Sundays and holidays. Both the rates and the method of computing them vary from city to city, but they are not substantially different from those given here. A rate card is always posted in the cab. Tip the driver 10 per cent to 15 per cent or add 500 to 1,000 lire to the meter rate. Be wary of cabs without meters or those whose drivers leave it up to you as to what you will pay. If the amount the driver asks is far above the meter price or if he clears the meter without your seeing it and asks a price which seems exorbitant, your best gambit is to threaten to call a policeman. The great majority of cab drivers are honest, but, human nature being no further advanced in Italy than elsewhere, there are always a few who will ask any price at all of a foreign tourist. The meter and other charges are for the use of the cab, not per person.

Horse-drawn carriages do not have meters, but they have established rates. Officially a half-hour ride costs 25,000 lire and a full hour costs 45,000 for two or three persons. A half-hour ride would cover about four kilometers. A longer ride, including a few tourist sites should cost, according to the rates, no more than 90,000 lire. These drivers are not obliged to post their rates, so if you do get involved in bargaining, let these figures orient you. If you reach an agreement, write it down on a slip of paper and show it to the driver if you are a little lame in understanding fast-spoken Italian numbers.

By city bus or streetcar. Buses and streetcars are an economical way to get about a city. The main points of the route are listed on the bus-stop signs. In Rome the ATAC (Rome's public transport system) bus map is available for 1,000 lire from the ATAC information booth in front of the station, or you can pick up other maps showing bus and trolley routes at most newsstands. With a good map and a little courage, you can move around the city easily by means of the public transportation system, particularly if you are careful to avoid the rush hours when trolleys and buses are crammed to overflowing. But remember that rush hours in Rome don't coincide with those at home. They are 8:00 to 9:00 in the morning; 12:30 to 1:30 at mid-day; 3:30 to 4:30 in the afternoon; and 7:00 to 8:00 in the evening. Within city limits, bus fares are 700 lire. A book of ten tickets can be bought for 6,000 lire at tobacco shops.

Bargain note. To get a good idea of the extent of Rome, the ATAC offers an excellent, inexpensive afternoon tour. See Chapter 4, WHAT TO SEE IN ROME.

In Venice, the steamers on the Grand Canal function as buses, stopping at regularly designated docks just as buses draw up to a bus stop. Fares are 1500 lire on most lines but 2000 lire on the faster Line 2. There is also an all-day ticket, which you can buy any time and is valid for 24 hours from the time of your purchase. It costs 8,000 lire. Line 5 is a circle line and a good one to take as an introduction to the city. It also costs 1500 lire. Gondalas are much more expensive, and it is a good idea to come to terms with the gondolier before you set out. The official price for gondolas, however, is 50,000 lire for 50 minutes and 22,500 for time over 50 minutes up to 25 minutes, after which you would automatically be charged for another 50 minutes. At night the rate is 60,000 lire for 50 minutes.

MONEY, SERVICE CHARGES, AND TIPPING

The Italian lire fluctuates a great deal in relation to the dollar and has recently undergone a significant depreciation. For the moment, the average is close to 1,370 to the dollar. Coins come in 10, 50, 100, 200, and 500 pieces. Bills are in denominations of 1,000, 2,000, 5,000, 10,000, 50,000, and 100,000 lire. Look at the numbers on the bills and count the zeros carefully. It's handy to remember that 7,000 lire is roughly equivalent to $5.00. 10,000 lire is about $7.15.

Sometime soon, Italy is expected to simplify its currency system by introducing the "heavy lire." When this occurs, the final three zeros of all denominations will be removed: 1,000,000 lire will become 1,000 lire; 2,000 lire will become 2 lire. Amounts less than the present 1,000 will be known as *centesimi:* For example, the current bus fare in Rome, 700 lire, will become 7 centesimi.

Money may be changed at banks, American Express offices, and authorized money exchanges. (The Italian word for such an exchange office is *cambio.*) Some hotels and shops in large cities will accept American money or traveler's checks, but they are understandably reluctant to accept personal checks. If you must pay for a restaurant meal with American currency, do not expect to get as high a rate of exchange as you would at an authorized *cambio.* As one restaurant owner explains, he is in the food business and not the banking business. The same holds true for taxi drivers, barbers, and small businesses of all sorts.

A service charge is added to all hotel bills and to most restaurant bills, its percentage depending on the category of the hotel or restaurant and the city you are in. At cafés, what you eat or drink at a table costs more than the same thing consumed at the bar, since the higher price includes table service. The theory behind all this, presumably, is to make tipping unnecessary. But waiters and human nature being what they are, things have never worked out logically, and tipping is still customary everywhere in Italy. There are two important things to bear in mind about tipping:

> Be certain that you know whether a service charge has, or has not been, included in your bill.

> Don't translate lire mentally into dollars when you are tipping.

If the service charge has been added to your restaurant bill, a tip of 5 per cent is adequate. In that case, if your dinner check comes to 30,000 lire including service, a tip of 1,500 lire is about what the waiter expects. If service was not included, a tip of around 15 per cent is customary. You can usually tell if service has been included by glancing at the bill. It will be the percentage dangling there at the bottom. But if you are at all in doubt, don't hesitate to ask.

Barbers, manicurists and hairdressers get 15 to 20 per cent tips. Tip

Colonnade of the Ducal Palace in Venice

taxi drivers 10 to 15 per cent (or add 500 to 1,000 lire to the meter rate). Theater ushers who show you to your seat get 500 to 1,000 lire depending on the price of your ticket. Railway porters charge 1,000 lire for one bag. The concierge of your hotel should be tipped from 2,000 lire up if he has given you any special services, such as obtaining theater or train tickets, receiving or sending packages for you, or making reservations. Chambermaids expect about 1,000 lire for each day's stay, and tour guides get 1,000 to 2,000 lire.

LEGAL HOLIDAYS

Italians love holidays, and they have many, both civil and religious. The unsuspecting tourist is frequently startled to find all the stores closed for a holiday that he has never heard of—and what's worse, on a day he had decided to devote to shopping. Official holidays are the following: January 1, *New Year's Day;* day after Easter Sunday, *Easter Monday;* April 25, *Liberation Day;* May 1, *Labor Day;* August 15, *Assumption Day* (called *Ferragosto*); November 1, *All Saints' Day;* December 8, *Immaculate Conception;* December 25, *Christmas;* December 26, *St. Stephen's.*

BUSINESS HOURS

The daily schedule varies from town to town in Italy, but the pattern is in general the same. Summer store hours in Rome, for example, are from 9:00 A.M. to 1:00 and from 4:00 P.M. to 8:00, with the exception of food stores, which re-open at 5:30 P.M. In winter, stores re-open in the afternoon at 3:30, close at 7:30 or 7:45. In Milan, stores re-open at 3:00, close at 7:00. Banks are open the year round from 8:30 A.M. to 1:30 P.M. and from 2:45 to 3:45 P.M. They are closed on weekends and holidays. Most museums are open from 9:00 A.M. to 2:00 P.M. others are open from 10:00 A.M. to 4:00 P.M. Almost all are closed Sunday afternoon and Mondays. The Vatican Museum is open from 9:00 A.M. to 4:00 P.M. in the summer and 9:00 to 1:00 in the winter and is closed Sundays except the last Sunday of each month. Barber shops (except for hotel barber shops) are open, for some reason, on Sunday mornings and closed all day Monday.

Generally, the further south you go, the later the opening and closing hours.

Food stores close on Saturday afternoons in summer and on Thursday afternoons in winter. All other stores close for one half day every week, but these closings are not uniform and tourists should check schedules before going out to shop.

CLOTHING SIZES

Any attempts to make Italian dress sizes comparable to American ones are only approximate, although you will occasionally see comparative size charts in print. One reason for the difficulty is that Italian clothes are not produced according to the standardized sizes used by the American garment industry; in fact, the Italians being individualists first and foremost, there is little attempt at standardization. In addition, Italian women are shaped differently from American women —they really are!—and since in general they are shorter, higher-waisted, narrower in the waist and fuller in the bosom and hips, clothes made to fit them simply refuse to drape gracefully over a long-legged, long-waisted American. Italian women still prefer to have their clothes made to measure, although nowadays more and more ready-made clothes are available. But remember that Italian merchants are often quite accommodating; if a dress or suit that you like in a shop doesn't fit you, you can ask to have it altered and it will be ready in a few days. Charges for such alterations vary, but they are usually minimal. In some shops it is possible to order a model made to your measurements. Remember, however, there are no refunds in Italy, although exchanges are allowed.

Shoes are even more of a problem, because, with the exception of the stock in a few stores like Ferragamo that specialize in American sizes, Italian shoes are not made in an array of different widths. The longer the shoe, the wider. The existence of a short, but wide, foot or one that is long, but narrow, seems never to have come to the attention of the manufacturers of Italian shoes. As a very approximate rule, an American size 8 is about an Italian size 39 in women's shoes. In men's shoes an American size 8 is about size 41. But this is so approximate that it is likely to be painful. The only workable method is to keep trying on shoes until you find two that fit.

Gloves, however, do follow the same size system used in America. Nevertheless, there is enough variation so that trying before buying is still advisable. Men's shirts are sold by collar size only and not by sleeve length. To find your Italian size, multiply your regular collar size by 2½. That is, a man who wears a size 16 collar in the United States would wear a size 40 in Italy. What Italians with long or short arms do about sleeve lengths is unknown.

Many stores display "*Prezzo Fisso*" (fixed prices) signs and bargaining is neither expected nor welcomed. You *can* bargain in the open markets—indeed, are expected to—but in stores you will get short shrift. If you make a number of purchases at one time, however, a storekeeper may occasionally offer you a discount of his own accord. But that is his privilege, not an obligation.

COMPARATIVE MEASUREMENTS

Italy runs on the metric system. Here are a few easy methods that you can learn to use in a few minutes.

It takes 2.5 centimeters (2.54) to make an inch, so to change centimeters to inches, divide by 2.5. A meter, which is 100 centimeters, is thus roughly about 40 inches, a bit more than a yard. To change inches to centimeters, on the other hand, simply multiply by 2.5. Twelve inches is thus 30 centimeters. Fabrics are sold by the meter and tenths. It's much simpler than juggling inches, feet, and yards when you get used to it.

For distance measurements, just remember that a kilometer is ⅝ of a mile. Eighty kilometers equals 50 miles; 100 kilometers is about 62½ miles.

To change kilograms into pounds, multiply by 2.2. If the scales alarm you by announcing that you weigh 60 kilos, it means you weigh 132 pounds. A husky 180-pounder comes down to an 82-kilo man.

One U.S. quart equals .946 liters, which is close enough to say that a liter is just a little bigger than a quart. Gasoline is sold by the liter, which is fine for toy-sized European cars but leads to higher mathematics in the case of big, thirsty American cars.

If you want to convert the temperature in the weather report from Celsius to Fahrenheit (or vice versa), all you need is a couple of easy mathematical formulas. To change Celsius to Fahrenheit, multiply the Celsius temperature by 9, divide the result by 5 and add 32. Example: 31° C. = 9 times 31 (279) divided by 5 (56) plus 32 = 88° F. To change Fahrenheit to Celsius, do the same in reverse—subtract 32 from the Fahrenheit temperature, multiply the result by 5 and divide by 9. Example: 68° F. = 68 minus 32 (36) times 5 (180) divided by 9 = 20° C. For easy reference, 0° Celsius is freezing (32° F.); 100° Celsius is boiling (212° F.). When you are feeling good, your temperature will be a modest 37° C., instead of the 98.6° F. you have been used to.

Winter sports—in the Dolomites and at Capri

SPORTS

Swimming is probably the most popular sport in Italy, perhaps because with the long coastlines on the Tyrrhenian and Adriatic seas, Italians are never far from good beaches of all types. The Italian Riviera, including San Remo, Santa Margherita, Rapallo, and Portofino, extends west and east of Genoa and is fashionable and crowded. Forte dei Marmi and Viareggio, just north of Pisa, have wide sandy beaches and many waterfront hotels as do the Adriatic resorts of Rimini, Cattolica, and Riccione. There is fine swimming on the Island of Elba and Sardinia and all along Italy's Southern coastline. Close to Rome there is Ostia, with its black sand and its crowded waterfront. Near Naples, the best swimming resorts are Capri and Ischia, reached by boat from Naples, and the Sorrento peninsula and towns along the Amalfi drive. There are many uncrowded spots along the coast of Calabria, with more tourist facilities being built every year. In Sicily the most fashionable spots are Mazzarò, just below Taormina and Mondello, near Palermo.

Skin diving is popular off the islands of Elba, Ponza, and the Treiti in the Adriatic; water skiing is a fixture at Capri. Windsurfing, an ideal sport for the usually calm Italian seas, is becoming popular everywhere. Tennis is played a great deal throughout Italy, and most towns have well-equipped public courts which charge by the hour, as well as private tennis clubs. Golf is becoming increasingly popular and good golf clubs can be found in all large cities and many resorts.

Skiing has thousands of devotees in Italy; the Dolomites and Italian Alps contain innumerable attractive ski resorts, equipped with the latest ski lifts, funiculars, and ski schools. Leading resorts in the Dolomites area are Cortina d'Ampezzo (1,224 meters high), San Martino di Castrozza (1,467 meters), Ortisei (1,236 meters), and Selva (1,567 meters) in the Val Gardena. In the Italian Alps, the leading resorts are Sestriere (2,033 meters), Courmayeur (1,228 meters), and Cervinia-Brueil (2,010 meters). About 2½ hours from Rome is Monte Terminillo (1,071 meters), which provides its own short season of convenient skiing. The new ski resorts in the Abruzzi Mountains National Park region are fashionable—two favorites, Pescasseroli (1,167 meters) and Ovindoli (1,375 meters).

In parts of northern Italy, skiing is year-round. Elsewhere, the season starts about Christmas time (the period from just before Christmas until about January 6 is very crowded at all ski resorts, and reservations are difficult to obtain) and continues until late March or even into April.

POSTAL RATES, TELEGRAPH, AND TELEPHONE

Stamps, being a government monopoly like tobacco and salt (strange combination though it may seem) are available not only at post offices

The Matterhorn—Mt. Cervino—as seen from Val D'Aosta

but also at tobacconists' shops. So look for the sign *Tabacchi* when you want to buy stamps. Mailboxes are bright red and are marked either *Lettere* or *Stampe*. Mail your letters or postcards in the box marked *Lettere;* the other one is for printed material only.

There is only one mail delivery a day in Italy, but mailboxes are usually emptied at frequent intervals. Letters usually take three days from one city to another in Italy. To other European countries they are automatically sent air mail whenever feasible, at no extra cost. For some reason, post cards and small packages to the United States sometimes take as long as six weeks to arrive. If you want your family and friends to know what you are doing in Italy *before* you get home, send your cards airmail in airmail envelopes. That way they will usually arrive in New York within eight to ten days and reach other cities a day or so later.

Italian postal rates are complicated. The important ones for the tourist to remember are:

Rates to Italy, France, Germany, Belgium

Postcards	450 lire
Letters weighing up to 20 grams	550 lire
Registered mail *(raccomandata)*	1,200 lire plus 2,000 lire extra

To the United States and Canada (Air Mail only)

Postcards	700 lire
Letters	1,200 lire
Registered mail	Regular postage plus 2,000 lire extra

If you want to have mail sent to you c/o General Delivery in an Italian city, it should be addressed to you at *Fermo Posta* of the city. There is a small charge of 500 lire for the service. In the larger cities you can, of course, get your mail c/o American Express, as generations of Americans have. No charge for that service.

Small packages weighing less than 500 grams (a little more than a pound) can be sent at low rates if marked *campione senza valore* (valueless sample). The rates for larger parcels depend on weight and distance to be sent and must therefore be figured out at a post office. If a package is to be sent to the United States, it should not be sealed.

Telegrams to the U.S. cost 968 lire per word. Telegrams within Italy cost 2,800 lire for the first ten words, with each extra word costing 100 lire.

Public telephones are most often found in cafés. Usually there is a yellow sign outside with a pictured telephone. To make a call, you either must buy a "slug" (called a *gettone*) for 200 lire or use 100- or 200-lire coins. Insert the coins or the gettone—being careful to correctly line up the grooves of the gettone according to the instructions on the telephone. Then, holding the receiver, dial your number. A new kind of pay phone from which long distance calls can also be made operates with a magnetic card. They cost from 3,000 to 9,000 lire and can be purchased in the Galleria RAS at Piazza San Silvestro, at Termini Station, at the public telephone center near the Galoppatoio in Villa Borghese, or at the telephone office at Corso Vittorio, 201, Rome.

ELECTRICITY

In Italy the electricity supplied to many homes and most hotels comes in two sizes—the normal 50-cycle alternating current, which varies from 115 to 130 volts, and the industrial 220-volt current used for electric heaters, refrigerators, and other heavy appliances. To prevent costly mistakes, plugs and sockets for the two kinds of current are different in Italy, but if you buy any electrical equipment, you should still be certain that you know what kind of current it is designed to use. You will also want to know if it will work on American current. (Some electric coffee machines, for instance, will, but many will not.) If you bring electrical gadgets with you from the United States, you will have to get a little extra plug to make them fit the Italian outlets as well as some kind of adaptor. More and more, especially in new buildings, the predominant current is the very high 220 volts.

HOTELS AND PENSIONES

Hotels in Italy are registered in official categories ranging from deluxe through first, second, third, and fourth—the category determining the rates charged. Nevertheless, there are certain differences from one part of the country to another in the degree of comfort to be found in hotels of each category. In large cities, and particularly in northern Italy, many second-category hotels are as attractive and comfortable as those in first category, and even the third-category ones are frequently comfortable and pleasant. In spite of the connotation the phrase may have for you, *second-category* does not necessarily mean *second-class*. Many hotelkeepers prefer to register their hotels in the second category simply because they then pay lower taxes and can attract more customers by charging lower prices. It is advisable to stick to hotels in the higher categories from Naples south, however, with the exception of Capri, where nearly all the hotels and pensiones are unusually attractive. In the Fact-Finding section of this guide you will find relatively few third-category hotels (*), and those that are listed are in areas where the level is generally high.

Pensions range in type from what are really small hotels to family boardinghouses. They cost less than hotels and are often patronized by people planning to stay in a city for a considerable length of time or those who are traveling with their family—and not only because they are economical, but also because they have a more relaxed and friendly atmosphere. Most pensions serve meals and usually require the visitor to take either all his meals (full pension), or breakfast and one other meal (half pension). Like the hotels, they are divided into official categories. Prices at a first-category pension, without meals, are roughly equivalent to those at a second-category hotel, but if you take all of your meals there, the proportional cost becomes even lower. Prices at a second-category pension are equivalent to those at a third-category hotel. Many pensions, particularly those in and around tourist centers, are very comfortable and most attractive. If you plan to be in a town for some time, you should certainly consider staying at a pension.

Daytime hotels *(Alberghi diurni),* one of Italy's contributions to traveling comfort, are found in most large cities. They have lounges, showers, toilets, checkrooms, barbers, hairdressers and other services. You can get a suit pressed, your shoes shined, and your money changed, and you can generally buy stamps and cigarettes. There is usually an *albergo diurno* in or near a main railroad station; others are often to be found in the center of town. They are perfectly respectable and much used, for example, by well-to-do people in town for the day for shopping or a social event.

RESTAURANTS AND EATING

When asked the difference between a *ristorante* and a *trattoria,* one traveler to Italy replied that a ristorante was a trattoria with delusions of grandeur. Both, of course, are restaurants in the American sense of the word. The trattoria is generally less expensive and less pretentious than the ristorante, but in many cases it is impossible to discover the dividing line. Certainly there is good food to be found in both. In the Fact-Finding section of this book you will find both types of eating places listed without distinction.

Breakfast in Italy usually consists of rolls and jam with coffee or tea. This continental breakfast is often—but not always—included in the price of your room at a hotel. But if you like heartier fare to start the day—fruit, cereal, or eggs—you will have to pay extra for it.

Italians eat their chief meal at lunch time, usually between 12:30 and 2:30. (Most Romans eat at 1:30.) The evening meal is served between

The coast of Sardinia at Porto Torres, north of Sassari

8:00 and 11:00 P.M. (Most Romans dine at 9:30.) In northern Italy, meal hours are generally a bit earlier. (Milanese, for example, generally lunch at 12:30 or 1:00, dine at 8:00 or 8:30.) In southern Italy, meals are slightly later. If you want to have dinner in Rome at 7:00, you may have trouble finding a restaurant that is ready to serve you at that hour, although many hotel dining rooms will be open.

Drinking Water. The water in most of Italy is good and may be drunk from the faucet in nearly all large cities unless there is a sign specifically stating *Acqua non potabile* (not drinking water). But in the country districts where you can't be certain, it still pays to be a little wary. Mineral water, which is available everywhere, is delicious, and you can get it in both fizzy and non-fizzy varieties. Many travelers like to stick to one or two well-known brands when they are traveling around the country, so as to avoid what used to be called "change of water" difficulties.

THE SIESTA

After lunch, Italians go home to rest and to stay indoors out of the midday heat. It's a pleasant idea and, particularly in the hot summer, a sound one. You will find that it makes a refreshing break in the day, and that after an hour's nap you can tackle your afternoon sight-seeing with morning vigor. Furthermore, since stores and offices are closed until three or four, you're not stealing time that could be used for errands!

REST ROOMS

Ladies' rest rooms are generally marked either *Donne* or *Signore.* (Note the significant E at the end.) Men's rest rooms are marked either *Uomini* or *Signori.* (Here there is an equally significant final I.)

ROME

Principal thoroughfares only.

Points of Interest

1) Ara Pacis
2) Arco di Costantino
3) Campidoglio
4) Castel S. Angelo
5) Colosseo
6) Fontana di Trevi
7) Foro di Cesare
8) Foro Romano
9) Mausoleo Augusto
10) M. Palatino
11) Museo Naz. Romano
12) Palazzo Colonna
13) Palazzo del Quirinale
14) Palazzo Spada
15) Palazzo Venezia
16) S. Andrea ai Quirinale
17) S. Cicilia
18) S. M. in Trastevere
19) S. Maria Maggiore
20) S. Pietro in Vinceli
21) Teatro di Marcello
22) Termini Station
23) Villa Borghese
24) Villa Medici

CHAPTER 4

WHAT TO SEE IN ROME

Rome (Roma) is one of the world's great cities—immense by almost every standard. It is the capital of a new and vigorous nation of 57,000,000 people. It is 3,000 years of layered history, above all others the city of classical antiquity. It is the heart and head of the Roman Catholic world of 628,991,000 people. Cities within a city—ancient and modern, pagan and Christian, known to everyone and yet to all still unknown—Rome stands alone among modern cities.

But Rome is not incomprehensible. With a population of 2,830,650 —not by any means the world's largest. Its population is a little less than that of greater Houston, a little more than that of greater Pittsburgh.

Rome is not elusive. Vast as it may at first seem, overlaid as it is by centuries of history, it still can be seen and remembered with pleasure even by those who have no more than a few days to devote to it. The Roman Forum against the background of the Colosseum; the Piazza of St. Peter's seen from the Via Conciliazione; the Sistine Chapel early in the morning before the daily crowds have arrived; the reposeful beauty of the umbrella pines in the Borghese Gardens; the indescribable softness of the Roman twilight as you look over the city from the Janiculum; the domes and spires of the city's four hundred churches spread below the terrace of the Pincio; the sudden realization of the actual reality of the bloody Roman spectacles that you experience as you look down into the arena of the Colosseum—all of these you can see and understand and hold in your memory of Rome.

You can see Rome well and pleasurably. One thing, and one thing only, you must remember: You will never feel the real grandeur of this great city if you move at a trot. The rules of Rome are simple, but they are absolute:

Slow down. Don't try to see all of Rome. It can't be done. Take the little time you need to learn the plan and shape of the city before you plunge in. Decide what is important to you. See that. See it properly. Let the rest go.

Rome cannot be summed up neatly in a few pages. Whole libraries have failed to capture the spirit of this eternal city. But for those who must choose between seeing Rome for a few days or never seeing it at all, here is a bare-bones outline guide to the city of the centuries.

As with any large city, the sensible way to begin a visit to Rome is to spend a little time at the start seeing it as a whole. There are, of course, several ways to go about that. First of all, there is the tour provided by the city buses (ATAC). These very economical tours leave every day from the Termini Station at 3:30 P.M. in the summer. Then there are the well-planned guided tours of Rome—particularly those operated by American Express, Wagons-Lits, and CIT. All of them cover much the same ground in four tours, morning and afternoon, for two days. If you have no more than a week to spend in the city, this may seem like an overly long introduction. It isn't, for in that time you will have seen the highlights and been able to choose with discrimination the places to which you want to return for a more leisurely visit. However you decide to explore Rome, the ENIT and EPT government tourist agencies with offices in almost all Italian cities and towns will supply you with free tourist pamphlets, information about festivals, concerts, museums, churches and excellent maps.

If you feel that you simply can't afford that much time, there are other ways to go about it. You can, for example, hire a car or a taxi and by planning your own tour of the high spots learn much about Rome in as little as half a day. Or, you can simply stand on the steps of the Victor Emmanuel Monument with a map and begin to see Rome from its center, the Piazza Venezia.

ANCIENT ROME

Campidoglio. Just off the Piazza Venezia behind the gigantic Victor Emmanuel Monument are two broad staircases, one leading to the *Church of Santa Maria in Aracoeli,* the other to the *Piazza del Campidoglio,* the Imperial square designed by Michelangelo. The statues at the head of the steps are the Dioscuri, Castor and Pollux. The marvelous equestrian statue that Michelangelo placed in the center is *Marcus Aurelius,* a masterpiece of the Imperial period (presently being restored). Left to right as you enter the Piazza are: the *Capitoline Museum;* the *Palazzo Senatorio;* the *Palazzo dei Conservatori.* These museums, second only to the Vatican collection, contain some of the world's most famous statues: *Dying Gaul, Cupid and Psyche, The Faun, The Capitoline Venus,* and *Boy With a Thorn.*

But even more memorable, perhaps, is the remarkable view of the whole sweep of ancient Rome below you.

Palatine Hill. Your guide for the Forum will probably go with you to the Palatine Hill. Possibly the site of the earliest Roman settlement, during Imperial times it became the richest and most aristocratic area of the city. Today trees and flowers grow among the few scattered ruins of all this great splendor. The *House of Livia,* the best preserved of the Palatine houses, still shows what a fine residence of the period was. The center of the hill is dominated by the ruins of a great and lavish palace built by Augustus and enlarged by Domitian. Erected on the foundations of many earlier buildings, it grew to be an immense and dazzling structure that was the wonder of its day. At the southern end of the hill is the *Hippodrome,* an oval stadium built by Domitian for sporting events. From here too, you have an excellent view of the gigantic *Circus Maximus* just across the Via dei Cerchi at the foot of the hill. Little is left of this great arena which was said to have held 300,000 spectators, but even as a ruin it is massively impressive.

The Colosseum. Huge, imposing, indestructible, this vast amphitheater is the first goal of nearly every visitor to Rome. Despite its size—it is more than six hundred feet in diameter across the longer axis, four stories high, and once seated over fifty thousand spectators—and despite the fact that it is a symbol both of the lavish splendor of ancient Rome and Christian martyrdom, it can be a disappointment to some, although most find it fascinating.

Built by Vespasian and Titus between 72 and 80 A.D., the Flavian Amphitheater occupied the place where a colossal statue of Nero once

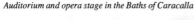

Auditorium and opera stage in the Baths of Caracalla

The Coliseum by night

stood—hence the common name. After the centuries of games and gladiatorial combats, the mock naval battles, and the sickening slaughter of the early Christians, this most famous of all Roman structures was deserted. One side was shaken down by an earthquake, and during the Middle Ages and on into the Renaissance it was, like most Roman remains, used as a quarry for building materials. Not until 1750, when Pope Benedict XIV declared it a holy place, was the plunder stopped. Since then it has fortunately been preserved and if you make the effort to see it in the perspective of its two-thousand-year history, it may more than any other monument in Rome evoke for you the staggering scope of time that confronts you in this city of the present and the past.

Arch of Constantine. Standing almost in the shadow of the Colosseum, this noble 4th-century arch is one of the most familiar and most photographed of Roman remains. Through this arch—it is really three in one —marched the conquering generals in triumph, and after them were herded their chained captives. The Romans seem always to have built literally on the past; many of the reliefs built into the Arch of Constantine were taken from earlier structures.

The Forums. Along the Via dei Fori Imperiali lie the great forums of Imperial Rome. Best preserved, perhaps, is the *Forum of Trajan,* built in the 2nd century and dominated then as now by the 130-foot *Column of Trajan.* This hollow shaft—with permission from the Ufficio A.B.A. del Comune, you can climb the spiral stair within—is decorated from bottom to top with an elaborately carved spiral frieze in which more than two thousand figures tell the story of Trajan's achievements. A golden urn containing the ashes of the Emperor once topped the pedestal, but in 1587 it was replaced by the statue of St. Peter which you see there now. The nearby *Forum of Augustus* and the *Julian Forum,* built by Caesar in 50 B.C. and the model for the others, are now somewhat less impressive.

The one area that reflects all that you have ever learned of Rome is the *Roman Forum.* Here you need either an experienced guide or time with a detailed guidebook, for in these few hundred square yards—carefully excavated and identified—is the visible key to all of the antiquities of this city. This was once the political and business center of the world. You enter by the *Via Sacra,* the Sacred Way, the main thoroughfare of the ancient city, and just beyond you stand on the paving stones of the *Argilatum,* the elegant shopping area where wares from every part of the world were displayed to catch the eye of rich Roman matrons. Here is the *Curia,* the building where the Senate met for several centuries; the *Comitum,* where the world's first town meetings were held; the *Lapis Niger,* the black stone that marks the legendary grave of Romulus; the *Umbilicus Orbis,* which marked the exact center of the city, and the *Miliarium Aureum,* the Golden Milestone, which recorded the distance to the capital cities of the Empire. There is the *Basilica Julia,* built by Caesar, and the *Aerarium,* the state treasury; and the three surviving columns of the *Temple of Castor and Pollux,* twin horseman gods; the *Arch of Titus,* which celebrates the capture of Jerusalem and the plunder of the Temple of Solomon; the burial grounds which were used eight centuries before the birth of Christ.

In the centuries after the barbarian conquest, when Rome had shrunk from a million and a half to less than fifty thousand burrowing and scrounging inhabitants, the Roman Forum was overgrown by weeds. Sheep grazed where Caesar had walked, and no one remembered even the name by which this spot was known. The whole history of Rome was buried in debris until modern archaeology revealed the glory that lived and walked and talked in this little space called the Roman Forum.

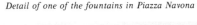

Detail of one of the fountains in Piazza Navona

The Baths. The ancient Romans all used the public baths, but they didn't go there merely to bathe. There were treatments to be had; hot, cold, and tepid baths; magnificent gardens, lectures, concerts, walls decorated with paintings, mosaics, and sculptures. *The Baths of Caracalla,* dating from the 3rd century, are well preserved. There you will see some of the magnificent mosaics that adorned the buildings. And there too, of a summer evening, productions of many fine operas are held. It is truly an experience to attend a musical performance in such an unusual setting.

The *Baths of Diocletian* have been variously used throughout the centuries. Within their walls Michelangelo built the church of *Santa Maria degli Angeli,* and other parts have been made into a museum which now houses some of the world's most famous statuary, including the famous *Venus of Cyrene.* Larger and later than the Baths of Caracalla, the ruins and the museum are near the Roman railway station and are called the *Museo Nazionale Romano.*

Theater of Marcellus. Near the stairs to the Capitoline is the theater begun by Caesar, completed by Augustus, and named for his nephew. It seated twenty thousand people and remained in use until the 5th century. It is now part of the 16th-century *Orsini Palace*—which has one of the most beautiful gardens in Rome.

Nearby are the *Temple of Fortuna* and the *Temple of Vesta* fronting on the Piazza Bocca della Verità (the mouth of truth) where also stands the church of *Santa Maria in Cosmedin.* At the entrance there is the head of a lion—it may once have been a sewer lid—and legend has it that if you tell a lie while your hand is in its mouth, the jaws will snap shut. If you happen to escape unmutilated, your guide will explain that the spell works only for Romans—a safe and convenient explanation which answers almost all deliberate liars.

The great ball above St. Peter's   *Roman road near Monte Cavo*

The Arch of Titus and columns of the Temple of Venus in Rome

The Pantheon. Built by the Emperor Hadrian to honor the divine ancestors of Caesar, and finished around A.D. 125, the Pantheon is perhaps the best-preserved building of ancient Rome. But even though it became a Christian church in the 7th century, it was still looted of its interior marble and bronze during the Renaissance. Its great dome, however, remains one of the architectural wonders of the world. It contains the tomb of Raphael, as well as those of the kings of modern Italy.

Mausoleum of Augustus. A great circular structure once covered by a hill of earth on which grew cypress trees, the massive mausoleum has been revealed by modern excavation. Within its crypt are the remains of three other emperors—Tiberius, Caligula and Claudius. Over the centuries the structure seems to have been used for nearly every possible purpose—warehouse, fortress, amphitheater, concert hall, and even as a vegetable garden. It is open every morning and from 4 P.M. to 7 P.M. during the spring and summer months.

Castel Saint' Angelo. Built originally as a mausoleum by Hadrian and used as a tomb by all the emperors until Septimius Severus, this grim and massive structure became a Papal fort during the Middle Ages, a very necessary adjunct to the Vatican to which it is still connected by an underground passage. In later years it was made into an infamous prison. It has been renovated by many hands over the centuries and now houses an excellent and interesting museum.

MODERN ROME

Piazza Venezia. You learned the first day you were in Rome that the whole city—ancient and modern—converges on this large and undistinguished square. You will pass through it dozens of times during your stay, get used to orienting yourself by that memorable confection, the Victor Emmanuel monument, and make friends with the ballet master who directs traffic through this maelstrom. Compared with the other squares of Rome, the Piazza Venezia is not particularly handsome, but you are likely to remember it with nostalgic affection for a long time.

Piazza del Popolo and Rome, at dusk from the Pincio

Half a mile straight down Il Corso from Piazza Venezia is *Piazza del Popolo,* considered by many the most beautiful in Rome after St. Peter's. Laid out in the early 19th century, it is an enormous double hexagon from which radiate three streets separated by twin churches, *Santa Maria dei Miracoli* and *Santa Maria in Monte-santo.* The piazza is dominated by the 78-foot Egyptian obelisk from the 13th century B.C. which Augustus brought to Rome. One facade of the gate through the ancient Roman wall was decorated by Bernini, the other by Michelangelo.

A double ramp curves upward from the Piazza del Popolo to the *Pincio Hill* and a magnificent view of the city with its old domes and towers. The southeast exit from the Pincio leads to the 16th-century Villa Medici with its celebrated gardens lying below the double-winged, twin-towered building. Just beyond, the Viale Trinità dei Monti runs between great oaks to the Piazza and Church of *Trinità dei Monti.* From the doorway of the church the 18th-century Baroque stairway called the Spanish Steps sweeps down to the *Piazza di Spagna* and the little boat-shaped fountain designed by Pietro Bernini, father of the more famous son. In the spring the steps are all banked with flowers and the flower sellers at the foot make the piazza colorful the rest of the year. To the left as you come down is the *Keats and Shelley Museum* in the house where Keats lived and died.

At the end of the Via Nazionale, opposite the Baths of Diocletian, is the **Piazza della Repubblica,** also called Piazza Esedra. It is memorable not only for its design and location, but also for the large modern Fountain of the Naiads which is handsomely illuminated at night.

The **Piazza Navona** is in the bend of the river near the Pantheon. From dark ancient streets you suddenly emerge into this great open space with its three immense fountains, two of them designed by Bernini. Once the site of the Stadium of Domitian, the oval area was for centuries used for races and other sports events, and during the summer was even flooded with water. At Christmas time a colorful open market and fair is still held there.

In the busy intersection in the **Piazza Barberini** at the foot of Via Vittorio Veneto stands the famous *Triton Fountain.* Nearby is the much smaller but charming *Fountain of the Bees.* Both are the work of Bernini.

Down the Via del Tritone and off to the left near the Quirinal Palace, the official residence of the president of the Italian Republic, stands the **Trevi Fountain,** surely the most famous in Rome. It is an enormous 18th-century wall fountain centered around a huge figure of the Ocean in a chariot drawn by sea horses. Millions of gallons of water pass through its vast pool each day. And so do hundreds of coins, for it is here, according to tradition, that the visitor to Rome drops his coin into the water to insure his return to the city. There is no evidence that the urchins who retrieve the coins deliberately invented the tradition or are responsible for its continuing popularity.

The parks of Rome are almost as well known as the fountains and squares. Chief among them are the **Borghese Gardens,** a huge expanse of gardens, groves, walks, and drives just beyond the Porta Pinciana at the head of Via Vittorio Veneto. Laid out as a lavish summer residence by Cardinal Borghese in the 17th century, it was purchased by the Italian government in 1902 and the grounds opened to the public. There are paths for cyclists and riders, grassy walks for strollers, mirror lakes, charming flower borders, beautifully tended formal gardens, an excellent restaurant. The zoo, one of the first designed to confine animals by moats rather than behind bars or in cages, is one of the great attractions of the gardens.

The *Borghese Gallery* is one of the really great collections of painting and sculpture from the 16th to 19th centuries. There are works by Bernini, Bellini, Caravaggio, Titian, Correggio, Raphael, and dozens of others. No amount of description can do justice to this superb collection. The Villa Borghese is one of the great sights of Rome and of Europe.

Looking across the Tiber to Castel Sant' Angelo

The Janiculum. Across the Tiber is the Janiculum, not one of the seven hills of Rome, but for you one of the most important, for from its summit, you get another of the views of the city that you will always remember. There you will see statues of Garibaldi and his wife, and be reminded again of what he did to unify the Italy that you see today. The history that you get here is important. The view is something that you will remember longer.

Villa Sciarra. Just beyond the Janiculum wall there is another park. You will never be taken there on a tour. Indeed, there are hundreds of thousands of Romans who have never heard of it. But those who know it think that Villa Sciarra is the most beautiful park in the city. It was once a private villa. Its walks, gardens, flowers, fountains, and statuary were chosen and arranged with excellent taste, and since the grounds have been open to the public, they have been maintained with what seems to be special care and attention.

Foro Italico. The site of the 1960 Olympics, this impressive collection of sports fields and swimming pools was begun as a pet project of Il Duce. Of particular interest is the Stadio dei Marmi with its collection of sixty statues. These statues, each donated by a different Italian city, are supposed to represent the various fields of athletic endeavor. The effect is sometimes a bit on the weird side.

EUR. On the southern outskirts of the city is the *Esposizione Universale Roma,* another of Mussolini's dreams. A grandiose project with dozens of buildings planned for an area the size of a small city, it was supposed to have been the site of a great world's fair in 1942, but Il Duce chose another path of glory instead. The new republic has continued the project, but funds have been scarce and the work goes slowly. Nevertheless much has been done and it is well worth the trip to see the impressive beginnings of what was to have been the city of the future. The *Hall of Congresses* is an immense and imaginative start.

Formal garden in the Papal Villa at Castel Gandolfo

Dome of St. Peter's   *St. Peter's from the Vatican gardens*

Trastevere. The area from the foot of the Janiculum hill to the west bank of the river is called Trastevere, literally "across the Tiber." It is the best preserved quarter of Rome as far as medieval architecture goes and is noted for its city planning. In the last few years, it has become a center for artists, young people and foreigners. Those who live there claim that this quarter was the site of the first Roman settlement. Be that as it may, nowhere else in Rome will you find people like this. These are the Romans that tourists seldom meet, and if you want to know the modern city, you should spend some time there. One expedition that will give you an opportunity to sample it is a visit to the *Porta Portese* flea market any Sunday morning. You can buy anything from busts of Mussolini to "genuine" Roman relics. Occasionally you can pick up really interesting buys, but the spectacle is the important thing.

THE HOLY CITY

Rome is, of course, a city of churches, ancient and modern, and if you spent all of your time visiting them you could still see only a few of the hundreds. You could profitably spend weeks in the Vatican alone. All that can be done here is to mention the most famous of all, the irreducible minimum which even the most hurried traveler should not miss.

Saint Peter's. The only approach to St. Peter's is through the *Piazza San Pietro,* a magnificent and inspiring introduction to the whole experience. Gian Lorenzo Bernini, the Renaissance genius who left his mark on so many places in Rome, spent a full ten years in perfecting the design of this truly majestic piazza. The great colonnades which enclose the oval space, the Maderna fountains on either side, the obelisk in the center—all contribute to the sense of grandeur. The monumental design and conception are indescribably powerful. But once you have felt the impact of the vision before you—have seen how all of this leads up to the steps before the church and the facade with its enormous columns and statues and to Michelangelo's dome soaring beyond—you

The facade and portals of St. Peter's

will have time to appreciate the details of this remarkable plan. When you stand on one of the little green stones that mark the two focal points of the piazza and see how the quadruple colonnade appears to have become a single row of columns, you will realize the extraordinary subtlety of this design.

St. Peter's itself is beyond description; it is to be seen and felt. There are, however, the numbers: The cornerstone of the giant basilica was laid in 1506; in 1626, the church was consecrated. Then, as now, it was the largest church in the world—561 feet long and 414 feet wide at the transept. The dome is 126 feet in diameter and it rises to a height of almost 400 feet. The building covers three and a half acres; each of the four piers that support the dome could contain a small church within its area; and a dozen or more people can stand in the sphere that tops the dome. But these are merely figures. The experience is something else.

To see this vast church from crypts to dome is the work of at least half a day and you will need either a detailed guidebook or a guide. Here is the briefest check-list of the things you will see: the five great *portals,* including the *Holy Door* on the right, which is opened only for a Holy Year; the great bronze statue of *St. Peter,* his toe almost worn away by the kisses of countless millions of pilgrims; the Latin inscription around the base of the dome, "Thou art Peter and upon this rock . . ."; the ornate spiraling columns of the *Papal Altar* designed by Bernini; the magnificent *Pietà* by Michelangelo in the first chapel on the right; the *Gregorian Chapel,* also designed by Michelangelo; the *Tabernacle* by Donatello in the Chapel of the Beneficiaries; *Pollaiolo's candelabrum* in the Hall of Treasures. There are the crypts with the tombs of the popes and, tradition claims, the tomb of St. Peter himself. There are the various stages of the trip to the top of the dome and at last the final fabulous view of Rome.

The Vatican. The collections in the Vatican museums and galleries are in size and quality among the very greatest in the world, and here again a detailed guidebook is essential. The *Vatican Picture Gallery Pinacoteca Vaticana,* alone is a matter of fifteen enormous rooms where you will see—to mention only a few of the most familiar names—works by Giotto, Fra Angelico, Bellini, Perugino, Raphael, Titian, Caravaggio, Murillo, Van Dyck. There are the several museums of antiquities—the *Etruscan, Egyptian and Paolino* museums, which are good, and the *Pio-Clementino* and the *Chiaramonti Gallery,* which include some of the most famous sculpture in the world in their collections— the *Apollo Belvedere,* for example, and the *Laocöon.* And there is the *Vatican Library,* an enormous repository of priceless books and manuscripts so huge that it has never even been fully catalogued.

Beyond all of this there are two apartments that no visitor should fail to see. The six so-called *Borgia Rooms* were decorated by one of the great painters of Italy, Pinturicchio. Just beyond are the four *Raphael Rooms,* which contain that painter's masterpieces executed for Pope Julius II.

And finally, beyond all of these treasures, is the *Sistine Chapel.* No one, of course, should, could, or does visit Rome without seeing the Sistine, but this fact in itself creates a problem, for through this one relatively small room pass hundreds of thousands of visitors each year. There is only one solution: be at the Vatican door before it opens at 9 A.M. and then, ignoring all else, go as quickly as you can to the Sistine Chapel. The few minutes you may have there before it is crowded will surely be among the most memorable of your trip.

Certainly nothing can be added to what has been said about the magnificent paintings you will see here. Michelangelo's *Creation* and *Last Judgment* are perhaps the most famous works of art in the world, and the frescoes by *Botticelli, Pinturicchio,* and *Perugino,* though they have been cast into the shadows by the overwhelming power of Michelangelo, are almost as great. You must and will go to the Sistine Chapel—but when you do, go early.

St. John Lateran. One of the great basilicas of the city, St. John Lateran was founded by Constantine and, as the Cathedral of Rome, is officially the principal church of the Catholic world. Revised and remodeled many times over the centuries, its façade is a monumental structure topped by enormous statues of the saints and apostles, its interior is rich and ornate. In a building in the Piazza di Porta San Giovanni are the

Holy Steps, brought here from Jerusalem centuries ago and believed to be the steps to Pilate's house up which Jesus walked on the day of His crucifixion.

St. Peter-in-Chains (S. Pietro in Vincoli). This 5th-century church houses the chains with which St. Peter was bound during his imprisonment. The church itself is splendidly adorned, but its greatest treasure is Michelangelo's famous statue of *Moses.* Commissioned for the tomb of Pope Julius II, the statue is one of the masterpieces of Renaissance art.

Santa Maria Maggiore. One of the four patriarchal churches of Rome (the others are St. John Lateran, St. Peter's, and St. Paul-Outside-the-Walls), Santa Maria Maggiore was founded in the 4th century by Pope Liberius. The present building is of various styles, having been completely reconstructed a number of times. It is notable chiefly because of its 5th-century mosaics and for its coffered ceiling—gilded with gold that Columbus brought back from the New World.

St. Paul Outside-the-Walls. The present church was entirely rebuilt during the 19th century on the site of an earlier building dating from the 3rd century, which was thought to stand over the tomb of St. Paul. The interior is rich and brilliant with its exquisite marble, superb mosaics and windows made of thin slabs of alabaster. The adjoining cloister dates from the 13th century and is beautifully preserved. It was in this church that Loyola took the oaths which established the Jesuit order.

AROUND ROME

All of Rome is not within the old city walls or even within the limits of the modern city, for that matter. Just outside—within an easy day's journey by bus or by car—there is a great deal that you should try to see if you have even a day or so to spare.

The Appian Way. *Via Appia Antica,* the most famous of all Roman roads, leads south from Rome. Though it was built in 312 B.C., many of the old paving stones still remain. In the distance, paralleling the road, are the ruins of one of the great aqueducts that brought the city its water for centuries. Both sides of the road were once lined for miles with tombs, and here too the early Christians came to bury their dead in the catacombs. There are many such burial places even within the city itself, but the most famous ones—the *Catacombs of St. Calixtus* and *St. Sebastian*—are in this area. Further along the Appian Way is the impressive *Mausoleum of Cecilia Metella,* built in the 1st century B.C. It is one of the best-preserved of ancient tombs, and since it seems to have been a favorite illustration in texts, most Latin students will recognize it immediately.

Along this same road or nearby are some of the most interesting and beautiful towns of the province—**Castel Gandolfo,** the summer residence of the popes, **Lake Albano, Rocca di Papa,** and **Frascati,** famous for its delightful wine. If you can spend only one day around Rome, you will do well to choose this area.

Via Aurelia. The modern road, following the route of the old, takes you through the center of the Etruscan country and west and northwest along the blue Tyrrhenian Sea. At almost any point you can turn left and in a few minutes be at a fine or famous beach—*Fregene, Ladispoli,* or further along, *Santa Severa* or *Santa Marinella.* This is the trip for you if you are looking for pure relaxation and a break from a too rigorous sight-seeing schedule.

Even closer, only a few minutes run by fast modern highways or by subway, is **Ostia** and the **Lido di Roma.** Ostia was for centuries the port of Rome, but during the Middle Ages was abandoned and gradually covered by drifting sand. Recent excavations have revealed the ancient city in a remarkable state of preservation. The Lido is, of course, the popular Roman beach—convenient, crowded, and lively—fine for a day-long excursion or for two or three hours of relaxation. Restaurants are excellent.

Anzio and Nettuno. Some twenty miles south along the coast is Anzio, where the allied troop landing was made in 1944. The city has been largely restored, the barbed wire is gone, but the beach is very crowded on weekends, and the water is polluted. But the immense British and American cemeteries are still there to remind you of what happened on this tiny strip of sand.

Tivoli. Twenty miles east of Rome on the Via Tiburtina is Tivoli, for many people one of the highlights of a visit to Rome. Near the town are the unbelievably vast ruins of *Hadrian's Villa.* Grass grows over the broken remnants of marble and brick, and Roman families come out here to picnic on a Sunday afternoon in what was once the greatest pleasure palace that an emperor could conceive. Here there were theaters, libraries, pools, and baths for literally hundreds of guests and servitors. Now there are sheep grazing among the ruins, but the villa is still magnificently impressive—more impressive, some people think, than it could ever have been in Hadrian's time.

In Tivoli itself the main attraction is the famed *Villa d'Este,* perhaps the most artfully and elegantly contrived garden fantasy in the world. Hundreds of fountains and a small forest of trees are so arranged that the eye is constantly fooled; what you see one moment has disappeared the next and another startling vision has taken its place. The gardens themselves are as enchanting today as they were four centuries ago when Cardinal Ippolito d'Este planned his gentle and amusing pranks with trees and water. At night it is all magnificently illuminated.

CHAPTER 5

WHAT TO SEE IN ITALY

To generations of travelers four cities have been the essence and image of Italy: Rome and its antiquities; Naples with its music and gaiety; Florence for the glories of the Renaissance—and Venice, the city of canals.

VENICE

Surely Venice (Venezia) is the queen of the Adriatic coast, a city of incomparable, almost unreal beauty. But fascinating as it is—and once you have felt its pervasive charm, you will be tempted to prolong your stay—you must remember that there is more than a single city to be seen here. Within a radius of a hundred kilometers or so there are half a dozen of the most interesting cities of Italy. And a short half-day's drive north will take you to the heart of the Dolomites, the weirdly spectacular peaks that mark the border between Italy and Austria.

When you plan your trip, it is best to remember that in the last few years Venice has become extremely crowded from June through August and is very hot then. April, May, September and October are the most agreeable months for a visit. If you have your heart set on lying back in a gondola watching the city glide past, there is still a right way to start your stay in Venice. You will most likely be arriving by the land route, which will put you on one of the banks of the famous Grand Canal, depending on whether you came by train, bus, or car. In any case, treat yourself and your baggage—which should be kept to an absolute minimum for maximum maneuverability—to a ride in one of the tiny canal steamboats called *vaporetti*. They are the Venetian equivalent of buses. Not only is this an inexpensive way to get to your hotel,

Gondolas and the Campanile of the Piazza San Marco, in Venice

it is also an excellent introduction to the characteristic easy-going pace of Venetian life. To do it properly, you should hire a porter for your bags at the outset and pay his fare on the boat—just so you will be relieved of the anxiety of watching for your stop. But if you are in a hurry to get on with your sight seeing then by all means take a hydrofoil, that is *motoscafo* straight to your hotel.

Once you are settled in your hotel you can put on comfortable clothes and shoes and wander over to the Piazza San Marco. There you look. Don't worry about time, just *look*. The next step is to saunter over to American Express or the EPT office (they are both located close to the Piazza San Marco) to pick up your mail and to get a supply of booklets and folders on the city. Then you take your little library and sit down at a table in one of the Piazza's open-air cafés—and relax!

The Piazza San Marco is the center of everything in Venice, the logical headquarters for a tour of the city. The largest square in the city, it is also a splendid place merely to sit and watch the world go by—and a fascinating world it is, in Venice. Even if you are a confirmed pigeon hater, you will enjoy the spectacle of the pigeons of Saint Mark's flocking to the square to be fed every afternoon at two o'clock. At night there are bands which play with much spirit a toe-tapping repertoire of old favorites. To the left as you face the church is the *Torre dell' Orologio* (the Clock Tower) with its two huge blackamoors who every hour strike the bell on the tower. At the right stands the towering 300-foot *Campanile,* a landmark with a great view of Venice. Built on Roman foundations in the 9th century, it collapsed in 1902 but was reconstructed ten years later.

Portals and mosaics of the Cathedral of St. Mark

The Cathedral of St. Mark, one of the finest examples of Byzantine architecture in Italy, was built in 829 to house the remains of the Saint brought from Alexandria by Venetian merchants. This basilica—hardly less magnificent than St. Peter's—is properly seen only with the aid of an experienced guide or a detailed guidebook. Addresses of experienced guides are available at the EPT office. The rich exterior with its five great domes, the superb façades with their magnificent mosaics and reliefs and their finely shaped columns and arches—these alone are worth the trip. But the interior is nothing less than breathtaking. The lower walls are covered with rare and exquisite marbles, and in a golden background overhead glow some of the world's most beautiful mosaics, notably that in the great dome at the intersection of the nave and transepts.

St. Mark's, built in the form of a Greek cross, *does* have two transepts. This accounts for the five domes, one for each arm and the great central dome over the middle of the church. The high altar with its lovely columns and rich canopy houses the remains of St. Mark. In the area behind the high altar stands the Pala d'Oro altarpiece, one of the church's finest treasures. Of the many beautiful mosaics, there are at least three that must not be missed: *The Creation of the World* and the *Fall of Adam* in the atrium, *Christ and the Prophets* in the central section, and *John the Baptist* in the baptistry. A visit to the Treasury with its excellent collection of Byzantine works is also definitely in order before you leave. All this as a bare minimum without even mention of the galleries, the chapels, the museum, the *Vault of Paradise,* or a masterpiece as great and famous as Tintoretto's *Last Judgment.* Take a guide and stay as long as you can. There is only one St. Mark's.

The Doge's Palace, a grand pink and white 15th-century structure to the right of the basilica, was the official residence of the Doge and the seat of the Venetian government. It still reflects the richness and importance of Venice in her days of glory. You enter the broad courtyard contained within the three wings of the Palace through a door called *Porta della Carta* (Door of Paper), so named because all official decrees were once posted on it. The spacious interior with its magnificent huge rooms is a museum of art and history where a guide is again essential. The *Scala dei Giganti* (Stairway of the Giants) leads to the second floor, where there is a whole series of rooms done by the great artists of the time, including Titian, Tintoretto, and Veronese. The Salone del Maggior Consiglio contains Tintoretto's great painting, *Paradise,* recognized as the masterwork of the Palace.

The Bridge of Sighs, one of the most famous and most photographed bridges in the world, connects the Doge's Palace with the dank and dismal prisons across the canal. It is called Bridge of Sighs because prisoners being led to their fate were said to have sighed as they had their last look at the outside. It takes only a single glance today to be convinced of the appropriateness of the name.

The Grand Canal is Venice's main street, and surely no visitor should leave the city without at least one gondola trip over its S-shaped length. To do it right, start at Piazza San Marco and go as far as the Palazzo Pesaro. Then have your gondolier take you through the smaller canals to the Campo dei Frari on the way back. It is the most fabulous gondola ride in Venice. For those on a budget, the *vaporetti* follow just about the same route and cost 1,500 lire. Among the dozens of notable sights along the way are:

Santa Maria Della Salute, on the left bank, is one of Venice's plague churches built by the famous architect, Longhena, in the 17th century to celebrate the end of an epidemic.

Accademia delle Belle Arti, also on the left bank at the foot of the first bridge over the Grand Canal, is the finest gallery in Venice, and one of the greatest art collections of the world. Its glory is quite naturally the art of the Venetian school—works by Giorgione, Carpaccio, Tintoretto, and Titian, to name only a few.

Palazzo Rezzonico, on the left bank again, has been preserved as it was two centuries ago. The palace, with its luxurious furnishings and many excellent paintings, is today the *Baroque Museum,* the top floor of which has a complete pharmacy of the period, a revelation to the 20th-century visitor. The palace was Robert Browning's last home.

The *Foscari* and *Pisani Palaces* are two excellent examples of the 15th-century Venetian Gothic style of architecture. The Foscari Palace, at the intersection of the Rio Nuovo, was the home of the Doge Francesco Foscari, the subject of Byron's tragedy, *The Two Foscari,* and Verdi's opera of the same name.

The *Rialto Bridge,* near the Pisani Palace, is one of the most famous of Venetian landmarks—and, by way of "The Merchant of Venice," one of the landmarks of English literature. Finished in 1592 by Antonio da Ponte, it soon became the center of the Venetian shopping district. Run down now, its shops and markets are certainly still worth a visit.

Ca d'Oro, the famous House of Gold on the right bank beyond the Rialto, is one of the loveliest of Venetian palaces. Originally built in 1440 as a private dwelling, it now houses the Franchetti gallery. Although overshadowed by the Academy of Fine Arts, the Franchetti collection is absolutely first-rate. Among the paintings: Mantegna's *Saint Sebastian* and Titian's *Venus at the Mirror;* among the painters: Van Dyck, Carpaccio, Guardi, and Tiepolo.

Palazzo Pesaro, a superb building on the left bank, is the masterwork of Longhena, Venice's most famous architect. Its Baroque exterior belies its present function. It now houses a gallery of Modern Art and a Museum of Oriental Art.

Palazzo Vendramin, a handsome Renaissance building, stands on the opposite bank just past the Palazzo Pesaro. It was here that Richard Wagner died on February 13, 1883.

Santa Maria Gloriosa dei Frari and San Rocco. If you turn left off the Grand Canal just opposite the Palazzo Vendramin, you can glide through tiny canals that few tourists see to the 15th-century Gothic Church of Santa Maria Gloriosa dei Frari. It has a memorial tomb for Titian, and also houses that artist's famous *Assumption,* as well as works by Bellini and Donatello. Just west of the Campo dei Frari is the church and school of San Rocco, important for its collection of fifty-six scenes from the Bible done by Tintoretto.

San Giovanni e Paolo, some distance northeast of Piazza San Marco, is chiefly noted for its four Veronese canvases in the lovely Chapel of the Rosary. On the square outside the church is the famous equestrian statue of the Venetian soldier, *Bartolomeo Colleoni,* by Verrocchio. Verrocchio was a pupil of Donatello, who also did an equestrian figure in Padua. It is interesting to compare the work of the master and the pupil, so keep this figure in mind if you plan to visit Padua.

The Lido is Venice's famous resort area—chic, wealthy, popular, and fashionable. Ten miles long and only fifteen minutes by motorboat from Piazza San Marco, it is, of course, a must for every visitor. Besides the fine Adriatic beach, there are dozens of luxurious hotels (cool even in midsummer when Venice itself can be sweltering) and for indoor sportsmen, a casino run by the city. It is also the scene of the International Film Festival held at the Lido's glittering Palazzo del Cinema, and if you are there in September, you can expect to encounter (or at least see) many of the great and beautiful of the film set who flock there for the event.

The Islands. Scattered through the lagoon is a twenty-mile chain of little islands, some remote little fishing outposts, others famous for their location or industry. A trip to some of the closer ones is certainly worth the half day it will take.

Murano is the island where the famous Venetian glass is made. Visitors are welcome to tour the factories and see the glass blowers practicing an ancient art that never fails to impress mere mortals.

Burano is the home of Venetian lace. You can watch the skilled lacemakers working their marvelously intricate patterns with the lengths of the material held on big cloth pillows called *tomboli.*

Torcello, somewhat further, is the place for you if you crave a few days of rest. This picturesque island is a favorite rendezvous for artists and just plain tired people.

VENETIA AND EMILIA-ROMAGNA

Treviso, a picturesque city about twenty miles north of Venice, is famed for its 15th-century walls and canals, which extend almost all the way around the town. Try to see the old city on Tuesday or Saturday when it is particularly vivid with the color and gaiety of the open markets.

Padua (Padova), located only twenty miles west of Venice, is a genuine bit of the Middle Ages. Its special glory is, of course, its excellent university, founded in the 13th century and still numbered among the world's great seats of learning. Another of Padua's glories—and perhaps its greatest—are the magnificent Giotto frescoes in the *Cappella degli Scrovegni.* They are the work of the young, confident master, luminously beautiful and certainly unsurpassed in any of his later works. And don't miss Donatello's equestrian statue of Gottamelata in the Piazza of the *Basilica of Sant'Antonio.*

Vicenza, another twenty miles west of Padua, deserves more attention than it usually gets. The birthplace of the architect, Andrea Palladio, whose work and influence led to the creation of the Georgian School, it is largely a reflection of his genius. The principal street is named for him, a number of his *palazzi* are located there, and his masterpiece, the *Basilica,* stands on the Piazza dei Signori. The Palladian design most favored by tourists, however, is the *Olympic Theater* at the foot of the shallow Corso Palladio. The permanent sets of this theater are in such perfect perspective that they create the illusion of great distance, though in actual fact they are less than six inches in depth.

Verona, the ancient city that was the setting of Shakespeare's *Romeo and Juliet,* is today one of Italy's larger cities, having more than a quarter of a million inhabitants. The center of the city is a charming complex of picturesque squares connected by streets that are hardly more than tiny passages. The *Piazza dell'Erbe,* once a Roman forum, is now a colorful square typical of this ancient city. The *Piazza dei Signori* boasts several impressive structures built by the ruling Della Scala family, the patrons of Dante. One of the principal points of interest to travelers is its remarkably well-preserved Roman arena, which is used for operatic performances during the summer. Elsewhere, you can see Romeo's and Juliet's family homes, the Montague and Capulet castles, and your guide may even point out a tunnel where the doomed lovers allegedly met in secret.

Ferrara is still another city from the past. The Este family ruled it from the 13th to the 16th century and made it a famous art and political center to which came many of the great artists and writers of the day. The *Castello Estense* is partially open to the public. In the castle you can visit the dungeon where Tasso was imprisoned for seven years. Patronage, it seems, was not always a pleasantly relaxed relationship. Also of interest in Ferrara are the *Schifanoia Palace* and the *Palazzo dei Diamanti* with its excellent gallery.

Parma, south past Mantua and across the Po River, is an old city with a great reputation for its animated criticism of operatic tenors. It will come as no surprise, then, to learn that Toscanini, who had a well-earned reputation for candid criticism, was born here. Correggio was also born near here, and Parma has many of his finest works—in the Camera San Paolo of the convent, in the superb frescoes of the Cupola of the Duomo, and in the National Gallery in the Palazzo Farnese, which contains his best-known work, *The Madonna of San Girolamo.* Parma was heavily damaged during World War II.

Modena, halfway between Parma and Bologna on the straight and ancient Via Emilia, is a thriving city in which the old and the new exist side by side. In Modena—which, by the way, takes the accent on the first syllable—the new includes the Ferrari automobile works (which make fine racing cars), and what is—or was—the highest concentration of Communists in Italy. The old embraces practically everything else in the city, most notably the imposing cathedral with its wonderful campanile and its superb and surprisingly earthy sculpture.

Bologna, called "La Dotta," the Learned, is all things—ancient and modern, carefree and profound. It is the seat of one of the oldest and most famous universities in the world, and its student body is known both for madcap pranks and solid learning. In a country where fine food is a commonplace, where eating is a well-developed art, Bologna is famous as a gastronomical center. At the crossroads of the Via Emilia and the route from Venice to Florence, it early became rich and prosperous, but it carried its success with an elegant style which it has never lost. It is today a charmingly disordered Italian city with miles of porticoes and arcades, two enormous leaning towers defying all the laws of gravity, dozens of notable palaces, the unique Church of Santo Stefano with its subordinate chapels, and several exceptionally fine art collections.

Roman Arena in Verona   *Cloister of S. Zeno in Verona*

Ravenna, the city to which emperors retreated before the barbarians, and the city where Dante died in 1321, is one of the great repositories of early Christian art. The *Mausoleum* of the empress, Galla Placidia, which stands near the Church of *San Vitale,* still bears remnants of 5th-century mosaics, as does San Vitale itself and *Sant' Apollinare Nuovo,* the old cathedral. All three are wonders of Byzantine art. Just outside the town proper is the grim and imposing Mausoleum of the Emperor Theodoric, built in 526. Though the city was severely damaged during the war, few of the treasures suffered. Ravenna is a golden, sunny town surrounded by fields and orchards. It can be seen in a day, but deserves more time if you have it.

Faenza is, of course, the town which has given its name to the world-famous faience ceramics. A shopping stop is most certainly in order. But the sight not to be missed is the utterly fascinating *International Museum of Ceramics.* The collection, surely one of the greatest ever assembled, includes pieces from all over the world and from many periods.

Rimini, a coastal town, is at once a modern sea resort and an ancient city rich in history. Here it was that Caesar's historic decision to cross the Rubicon was made, and here lived Paolo and Francesca, the unhappy lovers whose story Dante told. Its lovely beach and luxury hotels are surpassed only by those at the Lido of Venice. In the old town is the *Tempio Malatestiano,* which was severely damaged during World War II but which is undergoing restoration. This Renaissance building was built by the Malatesta family, the powerful and incredibly evil rulers of Rimini from the 13th to the 15th century.

THE DOLOMITES

The Dolomites are the strangest and most unusual mountain range in Europe—or in the world, for that matter. The weirdly beautiful rock formations, sheer needles and chimneys and towers, have been compared to many things including fortresses and castles and occasionally to the American Badlands. But they are truly unique, unlike any other sight you will ever encounter. Standing like a great impregnable wall between Austria and Italy, they are nevertheless crossed by many roads through the high passes and dotted on both sides with utterly charming resort towns.

Cortina d'Ampezzo, a little town tucked into the high folds of the mountains, is internationally famous. Site of the 1956 Olympic Winter Games, Cortina is popular as a winter and summer resort and is splendidly equipped with all the vacation appurtenances. The pinnacles that tower above the town on every side are an Alpinist's dream come true. If you are the less daring type of visitor, you will merely look and marvel. If you feel adventurous, take the cable car to Mont Pocol with

Cable car to the high Dolomites above Cortina d'Ampezzo

its magnificent view. This car is for seeing; the other, to Faloria, some 7,000 feet high, is for skiing. Both trips are terrific if not downright terrifying.

Bolzano, capital of the province of the same name and a city of 106,000 people, still retains much of its fascinating medieval atmosphere. In some ways more Austrian than Italian—the street signs are in two languages—it stands on the main route to the Brenner Pass which gives it a certain cosmopolitan aspect as well. Of particular interest in the town itself is the Via dei Portici, a delightful arcaded street with wonderful 17th-century houses. But attractive as it is, Bolzano is for most people mainly a jumping-off place for excursions deeper (and higher) into the mountains—to San Genesio by cable car, to the hidden historic valleys of Val Gardena and Val Badio, and to Merano.

Merano, a Tyrolean town that is only Italian by adoption, is a fashionable summer and winter resort, a spa, a sports center, and one of the most scenic spots in all of Europe. Once the favorite of European royalty, it is splendidly provided with fine hotels and restaurants and sports facilities of all sorts, from tennis courts to race tracks. As a spa, it has for centuries been famous for its "grape cure," and in recent years for its radioactive springs. It sits in the midst of history, castles, vineyards, and gardens. But what you will remember are the incredible mountains and the resorts—Avelengo, for instance—clinging to spectacular peaks thousands of feet above the city.

Trento, an hour's drive south down from Bolzano, is better known to most people by its English name, Trent. It was here that the Ecumenical Council of Trent met in the 16th century to strengthen the Roman Church against the growing Protestant movement. Trent is now a busy city of 99,000 but there is still much of the Middle Ages to be seen there. The moated *Castello del Buon Consiglio* (the Castle of Good Advice) built by the prince-bishops who ruled the area for eight centuries, is Trent's most famous landmark. It is now a museum with several rooms handsomely frescoed in the 16th-century style and an interesting collection of early Roman relics. The 13th-century cathedral is striking in its simplicity.

MILAN AND THE LAKE REGION

The commercial, banking, and industrial capital of Italy, the sprawling city of Milan (Milano) is situated in the precise center of the country's northern region, a bustling, proud, efficient metropolis that will seem at first un-Italian in its apparent dedication only to its mundane concerns. For centuries an important organizing force in resistance to the various foreign dominations that have afflicted Italy, it was Milan that first offered support to Mussolini and Milan too that fought the German occupation most savagely and consistently.

The city was badly damaged during World War II; many great buildings were wholly razed, and others gutted. In the years of peace, however, the Milanese have effected something like a miracle in their efforts to rebuild and refurbish the great monuments.

The Milanese are friendly, extroverted people. They live well, if a bit madly, amid a treasure house of art that compares favorably with that of Florence and Rome. Among the masterpieces which the city possesses, the one that is most often singled out, of course, is *The Last Supper,* the great fresco of that greatest of Renaissance men, Leonardo da Vinci. Also in Milan is the almost overwhelming collection of drawings by Leonardo, more than 1,700 of them, whose subjects alone—excluding their glory as art for the moment—are dazzling testimony to this man's incredibly wide-ranging intellect, his mastery of science, his intuitive understanding of problems that only recently have been solved by a purer scientific method. If only to pay homage to Leonardo, a visit to Milan is a necessity.

The vast *Duomo* is one of the largest churches in the world, and possibly the biggest of Gothic design. So intricate and involved is the decoration of this shimmering cathedral—begun in the 14th century and not completed until 1897—that one has an immediate impression of lace rather than masonry. You may find it rather too much, but you will be dazzled by the exterior. The inside of the cathedral is another matter, comparatively chaste and austere except for the magnificent 14th-century Trivulzio candelabrum, work of a great French gold-smith. You ought to climb to the terrace atop the Duomo and, though interrupted constantly by the pinnacles and spires and the famous gilded madonna, you will have a breath-taking view of Milan and the surrounding countryside—occasionally you can see as far as the Alps. (If you don't feel like climbing, there is an elevator.)

By all means visit the theater *Alla Scala,* better known simply as La Scala, whether the opera season is on or not. (It runs from December 7, the name day of Milan's patron saint, St. Ambrose, until the end of May; concerts are given in the fall.) The famous opera house, built in 1779, seats 3,000 people. Of particular note is the colossal chandelier suspended from the center of the carved and frescoed ceiling. For the amateur of opera and theater lore, there is an interesting museum connected with La Scala.

In the Piazza della Scala you will find the *Galleria*—similar to the one in Naples—a tremendous arcade completely enclosed in glass and masonry. This is the center of Milanese street and café life, with numer-ous restaurants where you may enjoy a *cappuccino* and watch the vigorous citizens in comparative repose. There are, as well, many shops in the Galleria.

A number of churches in Milan deserve at least a brief visit. *San Pietro in Gessate,* badly damaged in the last war, has been almost wholly restored now. It is of great antiquity, and although it has frequently been rebuilt, much of its beauty has been preserved. *San Lorenzo Maggiore,* begun in the 6th century, was much altered follow-ing a catastrophic fire in the 11th and restored once more in the 16th. Its shape is octagonal, with four large apses. Of the earliest construc-tion there remains the chapel of *St. Aquilinus* and some 6th- and 7th-century mosaics of great beauty and interest. The *Portinari Chapel* of the church of Sant'Eustorgio is one of the world's finest examples of pure Renaissance design.

The *Pinacoteca Ambrosiana* is one of the glories of Italy, both ar-chitecturally and as a museum. The building was begun in the early 17th century and is surprisingly severe in design. The museum itself is a repository for a collection of books, miniatures, drawings, and paint-ings; notable most of all is the so-called "Codice Atlantico," the 1,750 drawings by Leonardo, mentioned above. Here you will also find works by Dürer, Raphael, Bellini, Guardi, Botticelli, and many other masters.

Among the most impressive structures of Milan is the *Castello Sforzesco,* originally a fortress but considerably modified by the Sforzas— one of the great northern Italian families whose rise to power was only slightly less spectacular than that of the Medicis and the Borgias. Restored early in this century to its earlier form, the Castello Sforzesco is today much as it must have been at the time of its original construction, a fortified castle whose appearance suggests an impregnability it unhappily lacked at times. The tower in the center of the main façade rises to a height of 230 feet, and the outside walls are 12 feet thick and 100 feet high. There is a museum here too, notable for its collection of drawings and especially for its Chinese and Japanese art dating to the pre-Christian epoch.

The *Palazzo di Brera,* with its great library and magnificent Pinacoteca, is of interest to the art lover especially for its collection of paintings by virtually every master of significance of every Italian school. In addition, there are primitive Lombard works of great and unheralded beauty, and examples of Rembrandt and Van Dyck.

In the refectory of the monastery adjoining the church of *Santa Maria delle Grazie* is the fresco of *The Last Supper.* It was almost miraculously spared by a bombing that destroyed much of the rest of the building. The fresco was installed on a damp wall and has in succeeding centuries been restored very often, perhaps in the process losing something of its original luster. One of the most serene and splendid religious works of art, it still retains, however, its dramatic message of the Holy Communion. One may almost hear the words Christ uttered, "Drink this, in remembrance of me."

AROUND MILAN

Pavia. About five miles from one of the loveliest buildings in all Italy, the *Certosa di Pavia,* the town itself is noted for the *Church of San Michele,* an 11th-century edifice standing on the ground where Charlemagne was crowned king of the Lombards in the 9th century. The church has a splendid façade, but it is the Certosa that brings you here. Founded by Gian Galeazzo Visconti in 1396, this Carthusian monastery was nearly 250 years in construction, with cloisters of unparalleled beauty and fourteen chapels magnificently adorned. The statuary, the bas-reliefs, the marble door, the carving and painting and frescoes make this a great and harmonious masterpiece of the Renaissance. Here too is manufactured a liqueur well-known in the region. It—and also a perfume manufactured in the monastery—may be purchased after sampling.

Cremona. Known throughout the world of music for its magnificent string instruments, Cremona even today is haunted by the ghosts of the great Stradivari, Amati and Guarneri, whose violins, violas, and cellos are the finest in existence. Such is Cremona's fame that for many years makers of lesser instruments would paste pieces of a Cremona newspaper inside their products in hopes of duping a customer into believing them to be the work of a Cremona artisan. Apart from this artistic legacy, Cremona is known for its handsome 12th-century Romanesque *Duomo* and for the *Torrazzo,* the tallest tower in Italy, rising to a height of almost four hundred feet.

Mantua (Mantova). The cultural heritage of Mantua goes back to the elusive Etruscans, though not much more is known of its true beginnings than we know of its forebears. Important to see here are the *Church of Sant'Orsola,* octagonal in shape and built in the classical style, and the *Basilica of Sant'Andrea,* with its elegant campanile, begun in the 15th century. You will also want to see the *Palazzo della Ragione* and the *Palazzo del Podesta* with its adjacent tower dating to the 13th century. But of greatest interest to the visitor is the *Castello dei Gonzaga,* a complex of buildings comprising the Palazzo Ducale, the Castello San Giorgio, and the Corte Nuova, along with courtyards and gardens, which take up one entire side of the Piazza Sordello. The Ducal Palace is a treasure house of every important artistic period down to the present. The Castello, which contains Mantegna's famous room of frescoes, the *Camera degli Sposi,* is magnificent and worth as much time as you can give it. The Palazzo Cavriani is also of importance, dating originally from the 13th century, but rebuilt in the 18th. You should visit the Palazzo del Tè.

Mantua is historically and architecturally the most impressive of the smaller northern towns. Nearby are the three important battlegrounds of Montanara, Goito, and Solferino, as well as the village of Sabbioneta, a repository of many blessings in art and construction left by the house of Gonzaga, a family of almost legendary power during the Renaissance.

Bergamo. Founded about 1,000 years before the birth of Christ, Bergamo's history has been full of color and conflict. More like two cities than one, the town is divided by age and altitude. The older section, Città Alta, sits on the hilltop overlooking the more modern portion, Città Bassa. A funicular connects the two communities. Of particular interest in the old town is the *Baptistery,* classically inspired, originally a part of the nearby Basilica of Santa Maria Maggiore, but moved later on. The *Duomo,* founded in the 7th century and much altered, contains some first-rate paintings and altar pieces of exquisite design. The *Accademia Carrara* is thought to be among the best galleries of the north, housing an extremely catholic collection of paintings and art objects. It is in the lower part of Bergamo which is also the site of the *Palace of Justice* and the *Donizetti Theater.* The composer was a native of this city. Bergamo was the birthplace of Pope John XXIII.

Brescia. Perhaps of as ancient origin as Bergamo, Brescia was incorporated into the Roman empire at about 200 B.C. and retains relics of that great era. Its principal attractions, however, are of somewhat more modern creation, especially the *Palazzo della Loggia,* dating to the early 16th century, a graceful structure with a splendid arcade. The *Duomo Vecchio,* or Rotonda as it is more often called, is a Romanesque cathedral begun in the 9th century, offering comparative simplicity as competition for its more modern rival, the *Duomo Nuovo,* built by Lantana in the 17th, featuring a dome that is among the highest in Italy. The *Broletto,* housing the provincial administration, is of medieval origin and very handsome. There is a fine museum of painting in Brescia, particularly known for its medieval and Renaissance collections.

THE LAKES

The Alpine lakes of France, Switzerland, and Italy are among the most beautiful inland bodies of water in the world.

Como. At the southwest end of the lake whose name it bears, Como, a surprisingly large town of some 99,000 people, is the center of the Italian silk industry. (There are real bargains to be had here in bolts of silk, ties, scarfs, etc.) Because it is sheltered on the north by the Alps, the climate around the lake is semi-tropical; figs, palms, and other vegetation associated with more southerly regions flourish here. The town itself is gracious and extremely popular the year around with tourists. The *Duomo* is a lovely one, a blend of Renaissance and Gothic styles, with a façade made entirely of marble. Nearby is the *Broletto,* meeting-place of the town council, in vari-colored marble of the region of Carrara, with a campanile that was rebuilt in 1921. There are two museums, the Civic and that of the Risorgimento, in the first of which —among many curiosities, is a chariot believed to date to the 6th century B.C. This is the birthplace of the great scientist, Volta, and Como has erected a Temple in his honor near the Public Gardens and the lake.

You must, if you can, make the steamer trip around the lake. It takes ten hours and could only be better if it were longer. The boat has a restaurant and café.

Either by boat or car you ought to visit some of the better known resorts on either shore of the lake, especially Cernobbio, because here is the justly renowned Villa d'Este, today a very expensive hotel, but formerly the residence of Cardinal Gallio, who had it built in the 18th century. The building itself, the gardens and its situation on the lake combine to make it a glory.

Other ports of call for the steamer in its voyage around the thirty-mile-long lake include Torno, Argegno, Campo-Ossuccio, Tremezzo (with the rich and lovely Villa Carlotta and its fine treasure), Bellaggio, Menaggio, and others too numerous to name but too beautiful to be omitted on your trip here.

Lugano. Most of this beautiful lake is in Swiss territory, but there is no difficulty in crossing the border back and forth for short visits. The main Italian resort here is Campione d'Italia, wholly surrounded by Swiss territory and of interest primarily because of its casino, designed to lure Swiss francs from its neighbor. Small bets are accepted.

Maggiore. Longer by ten miles and somewhat wider than Como, Maggiore too is partially in Switzerland, the principally known Swiss town here being Locarno. Stresa is possibly the best point for beginning one of several steamer trips, although you can also start from Baveno. Be sure to see the Borromee Islands, and make the ascent to Mottarone; from the summit you will have a magnificent view of the lake and the curtain of Alps to the north of it.

Garda. The largest lake in Italy, Garda lies to the southeast of Como, but is climatically similar, semi-tropical. For centuries a resort for Europeans afflicted by good living, Gardone Riviera is well equipped with hotels and pensions. Other towns of interest around are Riva, beautifully situated, Garda (where the Princess Adelaide was imprisoned), Bardolino, and picturesque Sirmione.

THE RIVIERAS, PIEDMONT, AND VAL D'AOSTA

THE ITALIAN RIVIERAS

If you enter Italy from the south of France you will be following the coast along the ancient Via Aurelia, the Roman road that led to Gaul. The whole shore line, lying in the shelter of the Alps, is like a sunny, warm balcony above the Mediterranean. From the border to Genoa you will be traveling through the Riviera di Ponente (the setting sun), also called the Riviera of Flowers. Beyond Genoa you will be in the Riviera di Levante, the eastern Riviera.

The Riviera of Flowers is appropriately named, for in the mild, sub-tropical climate it is awash with blossoms the year around. Flowers line the road, fields are filled with flowers for the market, the markets are crowded with lavender, mimosa, and blooms of every color. The whole 200-kilometer drive from Nice to Genoa is a succession of resorts bathed by the sea and drenched in sunlight and color. The beaches are sandy, gentle, and warm; there is a plethora of excellent hotels and restaurants of every category; and the people are pleasantly expert in the business of catering to the varied tastes of foreign travelers.

Ventimiglia, the gateway from France, is an ancient town split into two parts—the Old Town and the New—by the Roja River. It has a fine archeological museum, and its Flower Market is a proper and delightful introduction to the major industry of the area.

Bordighera, brilliant with bougainvillaea and mimosa, is a hill side resort that has long been a favorite with British tourists. Just beyond the town is the cottage where Katherine Mansfield lived. Bordighera is famous for its palms and is the sole supplier for the Vatican Eastertide service.

Ospedaletti is a quiet, sunny, unostentatious town of picturesque palms and famous rose gardens and with one of the most spectacularly beautiful sea-view drives along the entire coast.

San Remo, capital of the Riviera Ponente and its largest and most popular resort, has for years been the luxurious center for the rich and socially prominent. It has scores of fine and fashionable hotels, miles of beaches, a yacht basin, an airport for private planes, sumptuous public gardens, two famous promenades—the Empress' Walk and the English Walk—and an expensively elegant air that has made it the queen of the Italian Riviera.

Imperia, with a population of 41,400, the largest city in the area, is an industrial center (olive oil), handsome on its hill but less popular with tourists than its more photogenic neighbors. From here to Genoa you pass through a dozen more resort towns—**Diano Marino** with a fine beach; **Alassio,** a modern resort popular with the international set; **Finale Ligure,** famed not only for its excellent bathing but also for its luxuriant gardens. **Savona,** the last major city before Genoa, is a maritime and commercial center.

GENOA

A city of 747,000, Genoa (Genova) is an industrial center and Italy's most important seaport. It has been neglected by most travelers, perhaps because many of them were too ready to take the old saying, "Genoese, therefore a merchant," too literally. Genoa is far more than shops and ships and factories. It is superbly situated, like a great amphitheater set against the hills ringing the port. It has a long and illustrious history back to the days of the Greeks and before. For centuries it was a great maritime power, the rival of Naples and Venice. It was the birthplace of Columbus, the starting point for the crusades of the Middle Ages, the seat of one of the most famous and influential old Italian families, the Dorias. In the winding streets of the old city, so narrow that two people can hardly walk abreast, there still remains more of the medieval atmosphere than there is in other cities that make much of it. Genoa is not to be missed; it is Italy past and present.

The area around the port has been described as colorful and picturesque. It is what all port slums are—and perhaps a little more; it is as blatantly disreputable and iniquitous as any harbor in the Mediterranean, with the possible exception of prewar Marseille. The waterfront —which was flattened once during the war and again by storms in 1954 —has been rebuilt. But it is still not for the innocent and the squeamish.

The upper city, reached by winding roads or funiculars, is a belvedere where one magnificent view is followed by another that is even more superb. From here you will see the whole city below you, the main section of it lying between two squares—the *Piazza Acquaverde* (the station, American Express, Wagons-Lits) and the *Piazza de Ferrari,* the shopping and theater district.

As in all large cities, there are tours, and if your time in Genoa is limited, you will be well advised to take one. You will be driven to the heights overlooking the city; visit several churches—Genoa has almost as many as Rome—where you will see works by Van Dyck, Velásquez, and others; climb to the top of the *Lanterna Lighthouse* with its twenty-mile view of the Rivieras; see the homes of Columbus and the violinist Paganini; be invited to drop your coin into a fountain which, like the Trevi, ensures your return to the city.

The Riviera of the Rising Sun (Riviera Levante) begins just beyond Genoa at Nervi and runs southeast to La Spezia, a little more than 100 kilometers down the coast. It is a fine Corniche drive all the way with the road hugging the shore and climbing the cliffs that jut out to sea. The coast changes here; instead of the long, gradual sand beaches, there are coves and promontories where the waves break against the rocks —the kind of shore that expert swimmers and sailing enthusiasts like.

Nervi, only a few minutes east of Genoa, is the oldest winter resort on the Riviera Levante and, with its parks and gardens and cliffside walk, one of the most enchanting. It has an excellent winter climate, no beach to speak of, but deep clear water off the reef that is ideal for scuba divers.

Just beyond Nervi are a series of sunny seaside villages—**Bogliosco, Pieve Ligure, Sori,** and **Recco**—less famous but no less beautiful than their neighbors. **Camogli,** not a resort but rather a little seafaring town huddled around a fine, colorful port, is an excellent base for those who want to explore the coast by boat.

Portofino, with its tiny bay and colorful square surrounded by lush green hills, has been a long-time society favorite. But even though it is regularly invaded by hordes of visitors, it still retains much of its charming old atmosphere.

Santa Margherita, a step away, looks out across one of the most beautiful bays on the coast. Lavishly equipped with all the appurtenances, it is crowded with yachts, sports cars, and young members of the international set throughout the season.

Rapallo, around the curve of the bay, is internationally famous—and lives up to its reputation. It has the ultimate in hotels, restaurants, and sports facilities and for many people is the climax of the whole Riviera. Beautiful, elegant, and aristocratic, it is still the favorite of those who seek the expensive best.

Sestri Levante, celebrated by poets from Dante to Byron, is famous for its fine sand beaches and for the promontory which juts sharply out to sea.

Levanto is a splendid modern resort dominated by a 13th-century castle. Beyond Levanto are the **Cinque Terre,** the five famous cliffside towns pressed tight against the sea. They are marvelously scenic, perhaps the best and most unspoiled part of this whole delightful coast.

Porto Venere is ancient. Once a Roman naval base for expeditions against Gaul and Spain, it has survived as an incomparable remnant of the Middle Ages complete with walls, gates, towers, and churches. Even in Italy, where the centuries mean little, Porto Venere is something special.

At the head of the gulf stands **La Spezia** with its beautiful gardens and its seaside promenade, the end really of the Riviera Levante. But just beyond, on the eastern shore, a few minutes away by bus or steamer is **Lerici,** famous both as a winter and summer resort, with its handsome villas scattered over the hillside. On its outskirts is a village called **San Terenzo** and a villa that should be known to anyone who has read English literature. It was from here that Shelley put out in a little sailing craft over a century and a half ago and met his untimely death in a sudden storm that capsized his boat.

Rapallo from the cliffside drive above the Gulf

PIEDMONT AND VAL D'AOSTA

Piedmont and the autonomous Val d'Aosta lie to the north and inland from Genoa. Piedmont was the cradle of modern Italy. It was the birthplace of the great Camillo di Cavour, and the other two leaders of the Risorgimento, Garibaldi and Mazzini, adopted it as their own. During the 20th century it has become the most productive, industrialized, and prosperous area of the country. Piedmont has everything that it takes to make a flourishing modern state—water power, fertile valleys, excellent communications, an alert and skilled labor force, and natural resources. It has more: fine food, good wine, a long tradition of skill in the fine arts and industrial crafts, and a spirit of resourceful independence that has put the people of Piedmont in the forefront of every advance in Italy in the last century.

Alessandria, the first major city on the way north from Genoa, is the second largest in the province. An industrial town and one of the most important rail centers of the country, it takes pride in two less commercial aspects of the city: the Renaissance art that it possesses, and the reputation that the women of Alessandria have for elegance and beauty. You are likely to remember the city for another reason—for this is the place where the famous Borsalino hats are made.

Turin, the principal city of Piedmont, lies beside the Po River in the foothills of the Alps. It is the home of Fiat, a gigantic industrial complex which dominates the city and has tremendous weight throughout the country. Fiat makes cars, buses, trucks, trains, and airplanes, and its products are sold throughout the world. A tour of one of the nine giant Fiat factories is one of the most interesting experiences of Turin.

But don't let the air of modern industrialization fool you. Turin is no Johnny come lately even in a country in which antiquities are commonplace. Turin's history pre-dates the Christian era and its tourist attractions are numerous and rewarding. Even the most reluctant sightseer will find it hard to resist the armor collection in the *Palazzo Reale* or the fascinating Medieval Village in the lovely river-front *Parco del Valentino.* In the *Academy of Science* there is an excellent collection of Italian and Dutch paintings (Rembrandt and Van Dyck, among others) and an Egyptian museum that is said to rival the one in Cairo.

Turin is a 20th-century city, the most modern and progressive in Italy. Because of that, Americans tend to ignore it—a sad, snobbish mistake.

Ivrea, some thirty miles north of Turin, is known for its beautiful river-side drive; its castles, including the great *Castle of Four Towers;* its ceramics; its fine food. But today it is most famous, perhaps, for the handsomely designed Olivetti plant where business machines exported to the world are manufactured.

VAL D'AOSTA

A few miles north of Ivrea at a little village called **Pont-St. Martin** —named for the Roman bridge across the Lys—is the entrance to the Val d'Aosta, an entrancing anomaly any way you look at it. First of all it is not a valley; it is a whole complex of valleys dropping down from the peaks of the Alps and joining in the main east-west valley of the Dora Báltea. Nor is it fully a part of Italy, for in 1947 it was granted a large degree of autonomy. Nor are the people Italian; they are cultur-ally and linguistically French. Almost nobody speaks Italian, though there are valleys in which German is the common, if not the official, language. The area is a modern industrial center—and at the same time is proud of its ancient heritage which goes back to pre-Roman times. From the tourist's point of view the most important contradiction is that though the area is called a valley, it is actually a mountain paradise with access to the highest and most beautiful peaks in Europe—Mont Blanc (15,872 feet), Monte Rosa (15,201 feet), and the Matterhorn (14,892 feet).

Some ten miles north of Pont-St. Martin is **St. Vincent** where the road swings west toward the border of France. The town itself is a well-known spa equipped with elegantly appointed hotels. It is better known for its casino which has been for years a source of income for the valley and a source of friction with Rome.

North of St. Vincent a few miles is **Breuil,** certainly one of the most spectacularly situated towns in Europe for it lies at the base of *two* of the world's most magnificent mountains, the Matterhorn and Monte Rosa. There is a whole network of lifts and cable cars to carry you up to the glaciers and craggy heights of these massive and sublime peaks —a "must" trip that few people are tempted to miss.

Aosta itself is due west of St. Vincent. Founded by Augustus in 24 B.C., it is called the Rome of the Alps because of its many ancient ruins. Particularly interesting are the *Roman theater,* the *Amphitheater,* the gates, and the *Arch of Augustus.* Industry? Aosta is an iron and steel center.

Twenty miles or so beyond Aosta is **Courmayeur,** the end of this tour and the end of northern Italy. And a magnificent end it is, for Cour-mayeur, one of the oldest mountain resorts in the country, lies at the very foot of Mont Blanc. Here certainly is the place to see and savor the majestic grandeur of the Alps. You can and will spend hours in the spell of this glittering mountain splendor. You can do more: a couple of miles away, at the very head of the valley, is the tiny village of **Entrèves.** There you can get the cable car that will carry you up to Col du Geant at 11,000 feet. And there, if ever, you will stand on the top of the world.

FLORENCE

Florence (Firenze) is the Renaissance. It is the city of Giotto, Fra Angelico, Da Vinci, Botticelli, Michelangelo, Donatello, and Cellini—the city of Dante and Boccaccio—the city of Savonarola and Galileo and Machiavelli. From this one small city on the Arno flowed the prodigious tide of culture that ended the Middle Ages and introduced the modern era. It is as old as Etruscan civilization and as modern as the sleek sports cars that snake through its narrow medieval streets. It is a living museum, a city that to generations of visitors has been the very essence of Italy.

In Florence, as elsewhere, the best beginning for the visitor is probably one of the popular morning-and-afternoon tours of the city. Tours offered by American Express, Wagons-Lits, and CIT are carefully worked out models of discriminating taste and modern efficiency. Best of all, they are not so rushed and hasty that you will feel footsore and mind-weary when you have finished.

After your first tour, you will want to return for a longer look at those things which interest you most. What follows here is a check list and refresher for this most important second visit.

Duomo. The Cathedral of Santa Maria del Fiore, one of the three landmarks of Florence, was nearly 150 years in the building, and when it was consecrated in 1436, was the largest church in the world. It is still one of the most beautiful of Italian cathedrals. Its huge dome, designed by Brunelleschi, is even now considered a remarkable architectural feat. The interior at first seems severe to the point of bareness. Nevertheless, it contains great works by the masters of the Renaissance—magnificent stained-glass windows by Donatello, Ghiberti, and Paolo Uccello, and in the three apses and five chapels memorable works by Ghirlandaio, Castagno, Luca della Robbia, and Michelozzi. Most interesting is the unfinished *Descent from the Cross* by Michelangelo in the first chapel.

Campanile. Designed by Giotto and begun in 1434, only two years before the great artist's death, this soaring bell tower was completed by Talenti and Andrea Pisano. Richly ornamented at the base, it achieves an increasing lightness and grace as it reaches toward its 270-foot height. The climb to the top is not for the weary or the easily winded; it is, however, broken by a series of fine views and capped by a panorama of the city that is unequaled.

Baptistery. Originally the Cathedral of Florence, the Basilica of St. John the Baptist was built about the year 1000, perhaps on the foundations of an older church erected on the ruins of a temple erected much earlier, and until the completion of the Duomo served as the Cathedral of Florence. The interior is austerely handsome but by far the most memorable work is the splendid *Magdalen* by Donatello. If it is neglected by visitors it is only because it is overshadowed by the great glory of the Baptistery, the magnificent portals by Ghiberti. In 1401 he won a competition for a design for one of the huge bronze doors and for more than twenty years worked to complete what is now the north portal. Twenty of its twenty-eight panels are scenes from the life of Christ and the others depict the Evangelists and Church Fathers. But it is the great eastern entrance which Ghiberti executed after 1425 that is his masterpiece. These doors, done in ten bas-relief panels portraying scenes from the Old Testament, are so exquisitely carved that Michelangelo declared that they were fit to be the gates of Paradise.

Museum of the Cathedral. Too often overlooked by visitors, the museum just behind the Duomo houses dozens of works of art which were originally done for the Cathedral, the Campanile or the Baptistry. Among them are many extraordinarily fine pieces by Donatello, Pisano, Luca della Robbia, Michelozzo and many others.

Palazzo Vecchio. This magnificent building—which, with its great 300-foot tower, is the second landmark of the city—was the political heart of the Florentine Republic, the seat of the Government. It is perhaps the finest existing example of the civic building of the Middle Ages. Revised and enlarged many times, its exterior is grimly imposing, its interior sumptuously ornate. Most impressive of the rooms is the *Sala dei Cinquecento,* the meeting hall for the Council of Five Hundred, decorated—as much of the palace was—in the 16th century by Vasari. In one of the niches near the entrance stands Michelangelo's *Victory.* There are many rooms to be seen—the *Studiolo,* which was the study of Francesco de Medici, the *Sala Duecento,* another council chamber, the *Apartments of Leo X,* and on the top floor, the infamous *Alberghettino* prison where Savonarola was tortured and from which he walked to his death in the piazza below.

Loggia della Signoria. To the right of the Palazzo Vecchio is the Loggia della Signoria, or Loggia dei Lanzi, an arched arcade which now houses

the famous statues that have become almost symbols of the city—
Cellini's *Perseus* and *The Rape of the Sabine Women* by Giambologna.

The Uffizi Gallery. Between the Palazzo Vecchio and the Loggia della
Signoria is the Uffizi Gallery, surely the greatest collection of paintings
in Italy and one of the three or four richest art museums in the world.
Many books have been written about the Uffizi and several excellent
room-by-room guides are on sale at the entrance. Even a simple list of
the names of a few of the greatest artists whose works are displayed
here is staggering—Cimabue, Giotto, Masaccio, Fra Angelico, Uccello,
Botticelli, Ghirlandaio, Leonardo da Vinci, Verrocchio, Michelangelo,
Raphael, Titian, Tintoretto, Del Sarto, Perugino, the Bellinis, Rubens,
Holbein, Dürer, and dozens of others.

A brief word of advice: The Uffizi, like Florence itself, is *too much.*
If you try to see all of it, you will merely confuse yourself. Decide on
one or two of your favorite artists or a period that interests you. Walk
through the gallery to get some conception of its richness, and from
there on stick to your choices.

Another word: This is the gallery for those who hate galleries. Try
it. Many a recalcitrant has succumbed to its charms.

And a final word: The Uffizi has the world's greatest collection of
Botticelli, one of the world's greatest artists. If you don't really have
a favorite artist, here is the place to get one. Botticelli, as he is displayed
here, is almost irresistible.

Pitti Palace. Largest and grandest of the Florentine palaces, Palazzo
Pitti was begun in the 15th century, later became the property of the
Medici family, who over a period of three centuries revised, remodeled,
and extended it to its present gigantic size. It now houses three great
museums, each of which would be the pride of any other city. The
Palantine Gallery has works by Del Sarto, Giorgione, Titian, Veronese,
Rübens, Van Dyck, Velásquez, Caravaggio, Murillo, and a host of
other famous masters. But just as Botticelli dominates the Uffizi, Raphael is the great glory of the Pitti. Nowhere else will you find a
collection of his works that even approaches this one. The *Gallery of
Modern Art* is a vast and famous collection of works from the 19th and
20th centuries. The *Museo degli Argenti* contains an immense storehouse of art works in precious metals, ivory, crystal, and stone.

The Boboli Gardens, just behind the palace, were created for Cosimo
de' Medici about the middle of the 16th century. They are perhaps the
finest example of formal landscaping in all of Italy. It is here that many
of the most memorable of the concerts of the famous *Maggio Musicale*
are held each year.

Bargello. A grim building erected in the 13th century as a residence
for the "Captain of the People" and later used as a prison—the Hall
of Arms leading to the courtyard was once a torture chamber, and the

yard itself was the scene of executions—the Bargello is now a magnificent museum. Among many works in the splendid Hall of the Council General are Donatello's magnificent *Saint George* and two *Davids,* one in marble and a later one in bronze. There are rooms dedicated to Cellini and della Robbia, and the Michelangelo room with his *Drunken Bacchus* and a bust of *Brutus.*

Ponte Vecchio. The "Old Bridge," as famous and much photographed as Venice's "Bridge of Sighs," has existed in some form or other for two thousand years. What you see now is the 14th-century version which, though the approaches were bombed out and the structure itself weakened, survived World War II. On top of the shops that line both sides —this is jewelers' and silversmiths' row—you will see a segment of the extraordinary half-mile-long enclosed corridor that Cosimo I built from the Pitti Palace to Palazzo Vecchio in the 16th century.

The churches of Florence are worth the visit in themselves, for they are filled with some of the greatest art of the Renaissance.

San Lorenzo. Begun by Brunelleschi and finished by his pupil, Manetti, in 1460, San Lorenzo, the Church of the Medici, is one of the monuments of this city of art. It has great and famous works by Donatello, Filippino Lippi, Settignano, and others. The *Old Sacristy* is Brunelleschi and Donatello at their best, but it is the *New Sacristy,* designed by Michelangelo, that makes this church the Mecca that it has become. Here are the tombs of the Medici that Michelangelo adorned with symbolic figures that are among the greatest of his sculptures—*Dawn, Dusk, Night,* and *Day.* Here too is his unfinished *Madonna,* which was intended to be a monument for Lorenzo the Magnificent. The *Laurentian Library,* which you enter through the cloister, was begun by Cosimo and, in its final form, was designed by Michelangelo. It is considered by some to be the most valuable collection of ancient manuscripts in existence.

Santa Croce. Built in the 13th century and renovated in the 15th, Santa Croce not only contains a great many works of art—chief of which are the Giotto frescoes—but also the tombs of many of the great Florentines: Michelangelo, Machiavelli, Galileo, Rossini, and many others.

Orsanmichele. Intended originally as a grain market and storehouse, St. Michael in the Herb Garden is famous because of the great statues that decorate its exterior—the patron saints of the Guilds who commissioned them. Among the greatest are *St. John the Baptist,* and *St. Matthew and St. Stephen* by Ghiberti, *St. Thomas* by Verrocchio, and *St. Mark, St. Peter,* and *St. George* by Donatello.

Santa Maria Novella. Begun in the 13th century and finished nearly two centuries later, this Dominican church is distinguished especially by two of the city's most important works of art—the series of frescoes in the choir by Ghirlandaio and the truly magnificent *Trinity* by the young genius Masaccio.

Santa Maria del Carmine. The original church was destroyed by fire in 1771 but fortunately the *Brancacci Chapel* was spared for it contains one of the priceless treasures of the Renaissance—Masaccio's great cycle of frescoes, the *Life of St. Peter.* Almost the whole life's work of this great artist is on these narrow walls. He had worked three years on this masterpiece before his tragic and mysterious death in 1428 when he was twenty-seven. Looking at this powerful series, you cannot fail to wonder what his genius might have achieved in a normal lifetime.

San Marco. This 15th-century convent, designed by Michelozzi, is severely simple on the exterior, but its interior glows with a warmth and beauty that is beyond description. In this building, where Savonarola lived for nearly ten years, Fra Angelico, one of the great artists of all time, spent most of his life in decorating the cells of his fellow monks. His wonderfully calm and beatific paintings adorn almost every wall and surpass even his great frescoes in the Vatican. In a city that boasts some of the greatest art collections of the world, San Marco is an experience that no visitor should miss.

When you have decided that Florence isn't a city of museums but a city of churches, prepare to change your mind again—this is also a city of palaces. The Pitti Palace, Uffizi, and Palazzo Vecchio are the most famous of these magnificent residences, but there are many others, truly palaces in appearance, as well as in name and history. *Palazzo*

San Francesco in Assisi   *Pisa's Cathedral and Leaning Tower*

Ferroni, in the Via Tornabuoni, built for the noble family of the Spini in the 13th century, still carries the air of a splendid medieval fortress. Probably the most perfectly classic of Florence's Renaissance palaces is *Palazzo Medici-Riccardi,* constructed at the end of the 14th century for Cosimo de' Medici and once the residence of Lorenzo the Magnificent. It remained the Medici headquarters until it was sold to the Riccardi family. The marvelously ornamented *Palazzo Rucellai,* elegant *Palazzo Strozzi,* and the *Palazzo Nonfinito* (the façade was never completed despite, or because of, a succession of architects) are but some of these architectural monuments to the men and families whose taste and power created the medieval and Renaissance grandeur of Florence.

THE HILL TOWNS

Florence is peculiarly captivating—so much so that you are likely to want to extend whatever time you planned to spend there—but don't skip the beautiful ancient towns set in the nearby hills of Tuscany and Umbria. Nothing should induce you to miss them.

Fiesole tops the hill overlooking Florence, no more than twenty minutes away by trolley. If it weren't next door to a greater city, people would be happy to travel miles to the *Cathedral* (a showcase for the works of Mino da Fiesole), the splendidly preserved *Roman Amphitheater,* the excellent *museum* with its exceptional collection of Etruscan and Roman relics, and the fine Medici villas which dot the hills around it. As it is, most people visit Fiesole to enjoy the magnificent view of Florence in the valley below.

A longer excursion west—plan to spend the whole day—will take you to **Pisa, Lucca,** and **Pistoia.** You will be fully aware of just how much the Tower of Pisa *does* lean when you climb to the top for the view of the *Piazza del Duomo,* called the "Meadow of Miracles," where there are other buildings as interesting as the Tower itself. The 11th-century *Duomo* is famous for its paintings by Andrea del Sarto and Ghirlandaio, the *Baptistery* for its great pulpit by Nicola Pisano, and the unique corridor of the cemetery for Traini's celebrated fresco, *The Triumph of Death.* More famous still is the view of all of these buildings around the airy, open piazza—one of the most photographed sights in all of Italy, surely, and still one of the most moving.

Lucca, an ancient town that still stands within its old walls, is the birthplace of Puccini, composer of *La Bohème* and *Madame Butterfly.* The *Cathedral* is something remarkable—inside and out. If you have hardly any time at all for this city, spend it in the Cathedral before the *Tomb of Illaria del Caretto* by della Quercia. There is no equal in all of Italy.

Pistoia has its green-and-white 12th-century *Duomo* and its *Campanile,* an ancient watch tower later decorated with terra-cotta work by Andrea della Robbia. Very much worth a stop.

If you feel that you can spend only one day visiting the hill towns around Florence, you have a difficult choice: you can go either to San Gimignano and Siena, or you can go to Perugia and Assisi.

San Gimignano, with its thirteen grim medieval towers, is a moment of the Middle Ages suspended forever in time, but **Siena** is the living representation of the Middle Ages and the Renaissance in Italy. For centuries, writers have been trying in vain to describe the mood, the atmosphere, the light and color of this remarkable survival. It must be seen—the unique shell-shaped *Piazza del Campo;* the massive 13th-century *Palazzo Pubblico* with its graceful and soaring *Torre del Mangia* that has become the familiar landmark of the city; della Quercia's beguiling *Fonte Gaia* in the center of the Campo; the magnificent *Cathedral* with its striped façade. There is simply no way to describe adequately this marvelous city of infinite peace and elegant charm. On two days each summer, however, there is everything but peace in Siena—on July 2 and August 16 when the picturesque and often riotous *Palio* is held. The parade of the officials and contestants in their 16th-century costumes, the blaring trumpets and the banners, the rising excitement climaxed in the wild horse race around the Campo—these too are worth traveling miles to see.

You will need a full, long day to see even the selected best of **Perugia** and Assisi in a single trip, but if that is all the time you have, by all means go. Perugia is another ancient city, serene, charming, rich with centuries of great art. This was the birthplace of Perugino, and you will find much of his finest work in the *National Gallery* with dozens of paintings by equally famous artists such as Piero della Francesca, Pinturicchio, Signorelli, Fra Angelico, and many others. The *Cathedral of San Lorenzo,* the *Etruscan Arch,* the ancient walls and their gates, the charming squares and churches—Perugia offers endless beauty at every turn.

Assisi. Assisi is St. Francis. The peaceful, loving spirit of the gentle saint who was born here dominates not only the great double church named in his honor but it permeates the whole mood and aura of this incredibly beautiful little city on the hill. The *Basilica of San Francesco* rises above the gate through which you enter the town and from the piazza as you look out over the violet, hazy hills of Umbria you will understand why Assisi's location has been called the most beautiful of any city in Italy. The lower church has a powerful *Crucifixion* by Cimabue and fine fescoes by pupils of Giotto. But it is the upper church that contains that great and glorious series of frescoes, the *Life of St. Francis.* Twenty-eight of the scenes were painted by Giotto himself.

Their indescribably beautiful colors, their wonderful child-like simplicity, and their perfect evocation of the spirit of *Il Poverello* all combine to make this great series of paintings as intensely human—and lovable, really—as the gentle and tender man whose story they tell.

And there is still much more to Assisi—ancient Roman ruins, the 12th-century *Duomo* which contains the baptismal font where St. Francis was christened, *Rocca Maggiore,* a massive 14th-century castle, and the lovely church of *Santa Chiara*—a contemporary of St. Francis who was born in Assisi and whose life is almost as interesting.

NAPLES
AND CAMPAGNA

Perhaps, as G. K. Chesterton said, "Nelson turned his blindest eye on Naples and on liberty," but in order wholly to escape the special quality of this rather incredible city he would have had as well to turn his deafest ear. For Naples (Napoli) assaults the senses; its sights, its sounds, its odors convey in a series of bold strokes the essence of the population. The Neapolitans are passionate about everything. When you first enter this violent city, you may very well have the impression of walking into the middle of a vast family quarrel—or, should the mood be right, a comic opera. As the saying is for weather in New England, if you don't like the atmosphere of Naples, just wait a minute; it will change.

Whatever you may have expected here, you will find the people the city's most vivacious attraction. They seem to have no homes, to live on the streets, to do nothing but talk (with much help from their arms and hands and heads) and to press one another forward on the crowded sidewalks, watch one another from one of the many cafés. More like Marseille than any other western city, Naples is ignorant of languor; but there is none of the sullen tension one finds in some cities. The vitality is all.

Naples is a pretty old city to be behaving like a five-year-old child. The Phoenicians are thought to have established a town nearby in about 1000 B.C., although the city proper was not founded until some six hundred years afterwards. Later, the Greeks, notably at Paestum, established here a culture whose classic relics are rivaled only by those of Sicily. During the period of Roman ascendancy, Naples and its glorious hills were a favorite resort for emperors, as was the island of Capri just a few miles offshore.

When Rome fell, Naples felt only a bit less bitterly the blows of the waves of barbarians who swept over Italy. Governed more often by foreign powers than by natives during the ensuing fifteen hundred years, the Neapolitans were torn by changes of authority that were mercurial in their swiftness and contrast. At one time or another, the city was the domain of Spain, France, and Austria. The confusion can hardly have been edifying.

In Naples itself, you would do well to begin your visit at the *Galleria Umberto* directly opposite the San Carlo Opera. The Galleria, a vast arcade with a roof of glass over a number of shops and cafés, is the center of Neapolitan life. Built in 1890, this teeming meeting-place can be the source of almost limitless amusement to the visitor.

Only slightly less important than the opera of Rome and Milan is that of the *Teatro San Carlo,* one of the largest houses of its kind in Europe. Rebuilt in 1816, after a fire had destroyed the earlier structure, its acoustics are as brilliant as its architecture.

Only a few steps from the opera house is the *Castel Nuovo,* begun in the late 13th century by Charles I of Anjou, one of the city's many foreign monarchs. It is a fine example of Renaissance design, much altered when the Angevin rule was replaced by the Spanish family of Aragon. Of special note are the vast throne room, almost of perfect cubic proportions (90 feet square with a ceiling 93 feet high) and the church and chapel.

Before making the ascent to the heights of the city, you should visit the *Castel dell'Ovo,* which is reached by a causeway leading from the Via Partenope. The castle was built by the Norman king Guglielmo I in the 12th century on the site of the villa of the Roman Lucullus. Used for centuries as a prison for political offenders, the structure now houses military offices. Moving northward along the Via Partenope, following the shoreline of the harbor of Santa Lucia, you pass any number of first-class hotels and restaurants, each with an impressive view of the port and the bay. The continuation of this avenue is the Via Caracciolo, one of the most celebrated walks of Europe, edged by the harbor and the Villa Communale—a long, public garden—and beyond the garden the Riviera di Chiaia with its beautiful buildings. In the center of the Villa Communale is the *Acquario* and the zoo, the former being one of the great aquariums of the world.

By the Funicolare Chiaia, which departs from the Parco Margherita, you come to the *Vomero* high above the bay. (If you can manage it, you ought to walk at least a part of the way, so spectacular is the view as you climb.) The view from the *Villa Floridiana,* with its charming museum and lovely walks, is perhaps the best of the city. A short walk brings you to the *Castel Sant'Elmo,* constructed originally in the 14th century and rebuilt in the 16th. The castle is now a military preserve, but may be visited by obtaining a permit from the military authority. It is from here that the noonday cannon is fired.

A short distance from the Castel Sant'Elmo is the *Certosa di San Martino,* a 14th-century convent redesigned in the Baroque style two hundred years later. Here is the hull of the ship of the Bourbon Charles III, and a wonderful refectory with much period furniture and works of art. The *Museo Nazionale di San Martino* contains an interesting collection of 17th- and 18th-century Italian art.

Down in the city again, you must visit the *Museo Nazionale,* established in the 18th century by the Bourbon Charles III to house an impressive family heritage of art and artifacts and now much augmented by more recent archeological finds both of Hellenic and Roman origin. Probably the most important single work of sculpture here is the huge Farnese Hercules. Overlooking the city is the recently opened *Capodimonte* Museum containing an important number of masterpieces of the Renaissance—works by Breughel, Masaccio, Botticelli, Raphael, Bellini, Correggio, Titian, Velásquez, El Greco, and others. There is, as well, a section devoted to antique mechanical techniques, many unearthed at Paestum and Herculaneum.

Of the Neapolitan churches deserving the attention of the visitor, the most important is the *Cathedral of San Gennaro,* containing the gold and silver chapel which houses the blood of Naples' patron saint. The Neapolitans say that, in times of prosperity, the dry blood turns to liquid twice a year. Of interest too is the Gothic *Santa Maria Donna Regina,* with magnificent 14th-century frescoes. In the convent adjoining the church of *San Domenico Maggiore,* St. Thomas Aquinas lived for a time, and in the church itself is the crucifix that is supposed to have spoken to him.

The food specialties of Naples include much that is familiar to those who have frequented Italian restaurants in North America. The pastas abound, as well as a notable fish soup that is reminiscent of the Provencal bouillabaisse. From Naples we derive the pizza, but the varieties here are much broader than found at home. The wines are delicious, both red and white; the fortified wines and vermouths are a staple of the cafés. The brandies are not the city's best point, but if you feel the need, most restaurants offer the French, as well as the native, distillations.

AROUND NAPLES

Campi Flegrei. These "flaming fields" were until quite recently actively volcanic, and the landscape leading to the bay is still curiously grotesque—as it apparently has been for centuries, for the area is described by Homer and, later, by Virgil. The land oddly seems to influence the sky which reflects an often ominous beauty. Particularly you should see the craters of *Agnano* and *Solfatara.*

Vesuvius. It is almost impossible for one to think of southern Italy without imagining at once the barren majesty of this volcano close to the shore. Standing about 4,190 feet above the sea today, Vesuvius has, in the last fifty years been diminished in height by nearly five hundred feet; it is still active, last erupting in 1944. That cataclysm demolished the funicular made famous by the rousing Neapolitan song "Funiculi, Funicula," but it is still possible to get close to the top (about 3900 feet above sea level) by chairlift from Pugliano, after which guides will escort you to the rim of the crater. The view of the Bay of Naples and surrounding shore are truly splendid.

Pompeii. Founded in the 6th century B.C., this town of 20,000 souls was inundated by the smoke and ash of an eruption of Vesuvius in 79 A.D. As nearly as can be estimated, some 2,000 inhabitants lost their lives. Yet so sudden was the occurrence, so quickly were the lives snuffed out, that when the city was rediscovered more than 1,800 years later it was found that the bodies of the victims had actually formed molds in the hardened volcanic ash. As Pompeii was slowly exhumed, it became a marvelously preserved ghost town, with its wall paintings, its baths, its amphitheater, its villas, and squares precisely as they had been on that frightful day. The original diggings were inept, but modern techniques make it possible to unearth and preserve the marvels that are still being discovered here. If you are interested, you can see the areas of current digging. There have been archeological discoveries of far greater cultural significance than that of Pompeii; but here is something unique, where life was extinguished almost in an instant. Still emerging from 2,000 years of silence, Pompeii is awesome.

Vesuvius and old lava bed   *The port of Ischia*

Herculaneum. Overcome by the same eruption of Vesuvius that submerged Pompeii, Herculaneum is not nearly so completely reopened as its more celebrated neighbor. An explanation is that the modern town of Resina is situated directly above a portion of its ancient predecessor. Another is that parts of Herculaneum are buried beneath as much as a hundred feet of volcanic ash, making excavation a slow process. Much, however, has been accomplished. Of special interest are the baths and the House of the Mosaic Atrium.

Sorrento. It is not hard to see why one comes back to Sorrento, a rather worldly resort nearly at the southern tip of the cape that separates the Bay of Naples from that of Salerno. Of ancient descent, Sorrento is distinguished not only for its fine hotels, restaurants and shops, but also for some notable buildings; the *Duomo* with its Romanesque façade, the churches of *Carmina* and *Sant' Antonio,* the 14th-century *Palazzo Correale,* and the lovely *Casa Veniero.* There is a pleasant museum from whose park there is a fine view of the bay. Naturally, you may enjoy yourself too by swimming, sailing, playing tennis, or fishing.

Amalfi. Even before you reach Amalfi, you are made aware of its beauty, so lovely is the approach along the Bay of Salerno, so beguiling the odors of citrus groves, the colors of the coastline as the road meanders for some thirty miles down from Sorrento. Amalfi itself was for centuries capital of an independent republic, maritime in interest, bitter enemy of Pisa and Genoa especially. Its present population of 6,000 is somewhat less impressive than the 70,000 it supported prior to the advent of the French dominion over Naples. There remains, nevertheless, much evidence of the great days—the *Duomo,* portions of which date to the 9th century, whose Byzantine inspiration is asserted by the bronze door that was cast in Byzantium. The Tables of Amalfi, one of the earliest codifications of maritime law, are found in the *Museo Civico.* The Cappuccini, now Amalfi's best hotel, was formerly a Capuchin monastery. You should plan to stay there for at least one night.

Ravello. On the heights above Amalfi, Ravello is one of the more serene of the villages south of Naples. Apart from its magnificent views of the blue water below, Ravello is noted for its having been the residence of Adrian IV, an English Pope who stayed in the Villa Rufolo, a splendid building begun by the family of that name in the 11th century.

Positano. Between Amalfi and Sorrento, Positano has for years been a haunt of artists and writers. It is a very beautiful setting in which to consider art or life. Suspended on rock above a bay that is more nearly a large cove, Positano used to be no more than a pleasant fishing village. Today, the artistic world has filtered in. Surprisingly enough, Positano has survived this invasion and remains one of the loveliest villages on this coast.

Roadside view of Amalfi

The bay at Sorrento

Salerno. In 1943, Allied troops established—with heartbreaking losses and very serious damage to the town—the historic beach head at Salerno. Most of the damage has been repaired now, notably that of the 11th-century Duomo with a celebrated atrium and a modern bronze door. There is also a fine provincial museum, featuring displays of antiquities found in the region.

Paestum. About twenty miles from Salerno is Paestum, the greatest Greek relic on the Italian mainland, with its ruins of Doric temples, celebrated by the classic poets. Little is known of the origins of this remarkable city, but its capacity to evoke wonder and mystery is limitless. Especially impressive are the *Basilica,* only a little bit less grand in proportions than the Parthenon itself, and the *Temple of Ceres,* which, in the early Christian era, is believed to have been used for a time as a church. Less awesome, it is thought by some to be even more beautiful than the larger ruins.

THE ISLANDS

Capri. The song that bears this lovely island's name has done it no favor —if only because Capri is mispronounced. (Emphasis is on the first, rather than the second syllable.) It is certainly one of the most beautiful spots on the face of the earth, a fact discovered by tourists in the 2nd century B.C. It is accessible by boat from Naples or Sorrento; you will probably land at the Marina Grande and go by funicular to the town of Capri itself. You ought especially to see the *Villa Iovis,* at one time the resort of the Roman emperor Tiberius, who passed happy hours here pushing his enemies off the bluff. Also of interest is *Villa San Michele,* at Anacapri, which Axel Munthe describes so vividly in his celebrated *Story of San Michele.* For a splendid view of the bays of Naples and Salerno, you should take from Anacapri the ride to the summit of Monte Solaro. Hugging the edge of the mountain is *Marina*

Piccola, sung of by Noel Coward, with amusing disrespect. A worth-while excursion around the island by boat will take you to the famous *Blue Grotto* with its luminous water, a source of enchantment, a memory you will cherish.

Ischia. Less worldly than Capri, and somewhat larger, Ischia is the more popular of the two offshore resorts with the Italians. It is, for one thing, slightly less expensive and a lot quieter. Its baths are said to be beneficial for practically every severe malady that flesh is heir to. Ischia too has its mountain, Monte Epomeo, from which one has glorious views of the island itself and the mainland to the east.

Procida. Smallest of the three bay islands, Procida has been the favorite resort of emperors and poets for centuries. Virgil and Juvenal, in ancient days, and Lamartine in the last century, agreed that Procida was delightful. You should, if you stop, see the Abbey of San Michele Arcangelo, notable for its Renaissance painting, and the nearby castle, which is today the Italian counterpart of Alcatraz.

SOUTHERN ITALY

Conical houses of Alberobello

The Greeks had a Latin name for it: *Magna Graecia.* Modern Apulia, Basilicata, and Calabria (respectively the heel, instep, and toe of the Italian boot) were in pre-Roman days one of the most opulent of Greek colonies. Today, the region is less popular with tourists than are other areas of Italy, mostly, one imagines, because of the somewhat trying climate and the extreme poverty of the people. There are, nevertheless, many rewards for the visitor, not the least of which is the fact that expenses are considerably lower here than elsewhere in Italy. Unlike many bargains, southern Italy is worth while. While accommodations generally are less luxurious than those in other parts of the country, they are good; the roads are excellent, many of them being fairly new.

APULIA

Vineyards and olive groves are typical of Apulia (Puglia), the heel and spur of the Italian boot. Until recently, other agriculture was sparse because of a scarcity of water, a condition much improved by the completion of an aqueduct. Consisting mostly of plains and comparatively low plateau, the Apulian countryside derives drama from its coloring—reminding one a bit of the drier portions of Provence.

The Apulians are wonderfully hospitable, proud of their land and especially of their recent resurgence. Romanesque churches are quite common, though many have been much altered. The food of Apulia is quite similar to that of the Neapolitan area, the wines heavy and heady.

Alberobello. Lying midway between Brindisi and Bari, about twenty miles inland from the Adriatic, this town of 10,000 inhabitants has a fairy-tale appearance. All the dwellings, commercial sites and even the first class hotel are of stone, freshly whitewashed and with conical roofs. Known as the *trulli,* these edifices preserve the traditional form of the straw huts of feudal times, which could be demolished quickly to avoid taxes.

Bari. One of the busiest Italian ports on the Adriatic, Bari is the largest city of Apulia, doing its major trade with Greece and the Near East. Attaining more than 90 per cent of its population in the past century and a half, the larger part of the city is modern and not especially engaging. There are, however, some lovely old buildings to visit. The great church of San Nicola and the Duomo, both dating to the 11th century and both considerably altered, are noteworthy, as is the Old City with its brilliant white houses.

Brindisi. The ancient city of Brindisium was the Roman gateway to Greece and the east. The southern terminus of the Appian Way, Brindisi gradually declined in importance—because of the growth of Bari as a port—until the later medieval period, when it served as a port of embarkation for Crusaders to the Holy Land. An earthquake in the 15th century destroyed the harbor entirely and much of the city too. Not until the latter half of the past century, when the monarchy undertook extensive restoration, did it revive once more. Of interest to the visitor are the museum, which houses many important and recently discovered Roman relics, a Norman castle of some distinction, and the Cathedral, which was begun in the 11th century, though altered since.

Lecce. Almost at the tip of Italy's heel, and set a bit back from the sea, Lecce is the second-largest city of Apulia and one of the most beautiful small cities in all of Italy, remarkable mostly for its Baroque buildings —the *Duomo,* the *Bishop's Palace,* the *Church of Sant'Irene,* the *Seminary.* There are also a ruined Norman castle and the remains of a

Roman amphitheater. The *Sedile,* notable for its magnificent Gothic entry, is today a museum of modern painting, and there are archeological treasures in the Castromediano.

The Promontory of Gargano. Until quite recently there were few roads and only primitive accommodations on this spur of the Italian boot, but there are now some excellent, beautifully situated hotels and transportation no longer presents a problem. Olive groves, vineyards and ancient chestnut trees cover lands sloping down from the immense, untouched Forest of Umbra to the clear waters of the southern Adriatic. For those who prefer nature touched by civilization, there are stupendous medieval monuments and Byzantine, Arabian, Romanesque and Norman ruins to see and charming small cities such as Foggia, Manfredonia and Pescara to visit. Boats for the Tremiti Islands leave from several of the promontory's ports.

Taranto (the emphasis falls on the first syllable) is the third-largest city of Apulia. Even by Italian standards, it is an old city, founded by the Greeks in 706 B.C., but nothing of importance remains of the days of Magna Graecia. Taranto was entirely rebuilt in the 10th century. The principal part of the Old Town is on an island that divides the Mare Grande from the Mare Piccolo, joining the modern city by a drawbridge. Of particular interest to the visitor is the *Duomo,* begun in the 11th century but repeatedly altered. The facade of the *Church of San Domenico Maggiore* dates to the 13th century and is very beautiful. Nearby is a Doric column that was part of a 4th-century temple. Called Tarantum by the Romans, Taranto has given its name to that rather lurid insect, the tarantula, and to the tarantella, a regional folk dance whose original purpose was to ward off the ill effects of the great spider's bite. The museum contains a fine collection of ancient ceramics.

BASILICATA

Basilicata is in many respects comparable to the mountain country of the Ozarks and Great Smokies prior to the intrusion of the automobile. It is Italy's last wilderness and for this reason alone is worthy of a visit. Accommodations are less than lavish, but in the towns of Potenza, Matera, and Metaponto, they are adequate if simple. A region of gorges and gaunt mountains, interspersed with forests and a few olive and citrus groves, Basilicata's countryside remains as it has been since the destruction of its ancient civilization. Wolves, wild boars, and other beasts still inhabit the wooded areas. It was of Lucania that Carlo Levi, celebrated anti-Fascist author, wrote *Christ Stopped at Eboli,* one of the better books to emerge from the period of Mussolini.

Potenza. With a splendid location, Potenza would be of greater interest to the visitor had it not been the victim of a devastating earthquake about a century ago. There do, however, remain several worthy points to be seen, especially the *Duomo,* rebuilt entirely in the 18th century, the churches of *San Michele*—dating to the 11th century—and of *San Francesco* with its notable wooden door. The *Museo Lucano* is of local archeological interest.

Matera. This small city is fascinating because of the rock on which it is built, out of which cave houses have been carved; still inhabited by the poor population of the town, they are among the most curious and primitive dwellings in all of Italy. There is a Norman *Duomo,* some Baroque and Renaissance churches, and the ruins of about sixty rock churches dedicated to St. Basil.

CALABRIA

Italy's toe is for the most part a mountainous area, insulated from northern, progressive Italy by the Sila range, and until recently few tourists ventured across the mountains to explore the coastal regions. The increasing number who do make the journey are rewarded by seas of rare beauty, waters of cobalt blue, deep violet and emerald green, bordered by land that is sometimes rugged and rocky but at other times fertile farm country. The olive trees are gnarled and ancient, three or four times the size of those that grow in the north.

Aspromonte, the mountain complex which overlooks Reggio Calabria at the very tip of the mainland, rises to a height of more than 5,000 feet at Montalto, providing an absolutely breath-taking view of the straits of Reggio, and of Sicily and its neighboring islands of Lipari and Stromboli.

The sandy beaches of Calabria's Tyrrhenian coast and the rocky promontories of the Ionic coast are Italy's newest playgrounds, particularly Maratea, Praia a Mare, Villa San Giovanni, and Copanello. And in winter, there is now excellent skiing on the heretofore unfriendly spine of the lower Appennines.

Reggio. Almost entirely rebuilt after the earthquake of 1908, Reggio is a splendid modern city of nearly 176,000, the gateway to Sicily. In addition to an interesting *Duomo*—reconstructed—there are some fine ruins of both Greek and Roman origin, as well as the towers of a 15th-century castle in the Piazza Castello. Nearby is the small town of *Scilla* (the Scylla of Homer) and—of course—on the opposite shore in Sicily is *Charybdis.* In the archeological museum of Reggio are now housed the recently restored Warriors of Riace, two beautiful bronze statues, which were found near the fishing village of Riace by a diver in 1972, after nearly two thousand years of repose in the bottom of the sea.

Cosenza. Picturesque in its situation at the confluence of the Crati and Busento, Cosenza is notable for its castle—built by the ubiquitous

Frederick II of Swabia—which has a commanding view of the surrounding area it, and for the *Duomo,* built in the 12th century, but remodeled in the Baroque style in the mid-18th century. The *Church of San Francesco d'Assisi* is remarkable for its beautiful medieval cloister.

Catanzaro. Ancient Catacium, Catanzaro is back from the sea a few miles, overlooking two rivers, the Musofalo and the Fiumarella. Its cathedral, while not of great antiquity, is quite lovely, and possesses some distinguished painting salvaged from its predecessor, which was destroyed in the earthquake of 1783. There is also the ruin of a Norman castle built here in the 11th century.

SICILY AND
SARDINIA

Just off the toe of the Italian boot lies Sicily (Sicilia)—the Island of the Sun, the Golden Island of myth and legend. By far the largest of the Mediterranean islands—more than 225 miles wide on its longest side (the northern) and over 600 miles around—it is within easy reach of the mainland. You can ferry across the Straits of Messina (which literally separate Scylla and Charybdis), or fly from Rome or Naples. Which ever way you choose, the trip will not take much more than an hour.

You will find that Sicily is an adventure into time and beauty unlike anything you have ever known. Though it has been popular with travelers for centuries, and has garnered glowing compliments from visitors all the way from Aeschylus and Plato to Goethe and D. H. Lawrence, it is still less crowded than the rest of Italy. In recent years more tourists rediscovered Sicily but even popularity cannot obscure the charms of this island of flowers—its perfect climate, the mountain-to-sea beauty of its landscape, Greek temples that make the monuments of Rome seem almost new, and a most remarkable people who are the synthesis of at least half a dozen civilizations.

Of the earliest inhabitants of the island—the Siculi and the Sicani—little is known except that they gave the island its name and left burial caves in many regions. From the beginning, Sicily has had a succession of masters. First came the Phoenicians, who settled in Palermo, and then the Carthagenians, who occupied the southern coast. The golden age of Sicily began in the 8th century B.C. with the founding of the great Greek cities there. As the Roman Empire rose to power, Sicily became a colony, and when Rome fell before the barbarian attacks, the island was lost to Byzantium. In the 9th century A.D. the Arabs captured and held it for two centuries. The Normans dislodged them in 1060 and Roger I became the first king. He was followed by the Swabian Frederick II and the unhappy vassalage under the Bourbons and the Spanish house of Aragon which was ended by the Garibaldi liberation of 1860.

Sicily was the crossroads between Europe and Africa, between Greece and Rome, between Christianity and Islam. And its whole background is visible and tangible today—in the extraordinary group of temples at Agrigento, in the fine National Museum at Palermo, in the Norman-Arab style of the cathedrals at Monreale and Cefalù, in that dazzling golden jewel of Byzantine mosaic art, the Palatine Chapel of Palermo, to many minds the most beautiful in the world.

For the visitor the delights and surprises of Sicily seem almost endless. It is the land of mythology: the *Riviera dei Ciclopi* where the enraged Cyclops threw giant rocks at the fleeing Ulysses; the mysterious Lake Pergusa where Pluto captured Proserpine and carried her off to Hades; the spot where Daedalus winged down after his flight from Crete. This is the country where the donkey carts are painted with elaborate historical scenes, where taboos and superstitions are the daily guides of many people, where religious festivals are colored with ancient rites and symbols.

Columns in Monreale cloister   *Interior of Palatine Chapel*

Even with all of this the Sicilians themselves are perhaps the island's greatest attraction. Fiercely proud—they will remind you that theirs was a great civilization while the Florentines were still living in caves —they are also extremely polite, almost courtly. They are a warm, emotional people—and almost without exception they love Americans. Through all the years of emigration the United States has been the Promised Land to Sicilians. Almost everybody has uncles and cousins scattered the length of America and you will be asked again and again if you know any of them. Once in a great while it happens that a visitor *does* know one of the myriad relatives, and if it should happen to you, be prepared to be swept into the bosom of the family and made the center of an impromptu fiesta.

Sicily is becoming increasingly popular, especially with Americans, and wherever you go nowadays you will find excellent accommodations —good restaurants, modern hotels, motels (notably the Jolly chain), comfortable pensions, tourist villages with housekeeping facilities. And prices for comparable food and lodging are much lower in Sicily than on the mainland.

SEEING SICILY

Palermo. Capital and largest city of Sicily, Palermo is sheltered in the curve of the *Conca d'Oro* (the Golden Shell), a sweeping deep-sea harbor lying at the foot of dramatic Monte Pellegrino. With its fine setting, its elegant streets and garden squares, its luxuriant parks and villas, it is the cultural center of the island—as it has been ever since the Arabs made it their capital in the 9th century. Meeting place of the East and West and a fascinating mixture of many cultures, it fully deserves the name "Pearl of the Mediterranean."

Badly damaged though it was during the last war, it still has many buildings of artistic and historical interest—among them at least two of the most beautiful structures in all of Italy, the Palace of the Norman Kings, and the Cathedral at Monreale, just outside the city.

The 12th-century *Duomo* is powerful and impressive, its grandeur in keeping with the half dozen tombs of kings and emperors within. But the noblest building in the city is surely the *Palazzo dei Re' Normanni,* the Palace of the Norman Kings, which is now the seat of the Sicilian parliament. Arab in its beginning, it was later enlarged and decorated by Moorish artists in the employ of the Norman rulers. The glory of the building is the superb *Cappella Palatina,* the Palatine Chapel. Built in the 12th century, it is one of the world's great examples of Arab art. From top to bottom—walls, ceiling, columns, arches—it blazes with magnificent red and gold mosaics that are pure magic. If you see nothing else in Palermo, don't miss this one exquisite experience.

Many buildings in Palermo were designed by Arab craftsmen. One

Palermo and its harbor from Monte Pellegrino

of them is *San Giovanni degli Ermitti,* St. John of the Hermits, with its striking red domes. The adjacent cloister, lined with a row of double columns, and the fine Oriental garden with its rare tropical plants are other facets of Sicilian grace and charm.

La Martorana is in structure a Norman church. But the mosaics inside are frankly Byzantine and the fine 12th-century bell tower is an extraordinary blend of Norman solidity and Arab fancy. *San Cataldo,* another 12th-century church, with its fine mosaic floor and its three domes has much the same Arab air, and the monastic buildings clustered around it make it seem impressively medieval.

Monreale. Only three or four miles from the heart of the city, Monreale is really part of Palermo—and perhaps its most memorable part, for here, on a majestic height overlooking the harbor, stands one of the great cathedrals of the world. Like most of the churches on the island, it is basically Norman in its structure, though built by 12th-century Byzantine and Sicilian artists and artisans. The whole interior is alive with mosaics—130 scenes from the Old Testament and the New— possibly the greatest of their kind in the world. Equally magnificent are the cloisters with their two hundred twin columns, each marvelously and individually adorned with mosaics and capitals of infinite variety. And, as if this weren't enough, from the cloisters you look down over the whole city and out across the blue-green beauty of the Conca d'Oro, one of the oldest and most beautiful harbors in the world.

There is much more to Palermo—palaces, churches, catacombs, piazzas, fountains—but these two, the Palatine Chapel and Monreale, are two high points of human achievement that nobody who passes through this city should miss.

Piana degli Albanesi, a mountain town only a few miles from Palermo, is another side of Sicilian life. Founded by Albanian immigrants in the 15th century, it is still a pocket of alien culture. The people speak their ancient dialect, preserve their Eastern customs and church rites, wear their colorful and elaborate costumes for all festivals.

Cefalù. Going east along the fine beaches of the northern coast, nearly a third of the way to Messina, is Cefalù, an ancient little town that looks out to the sea from a great rocky eminence. It has a good beach and good accommodations for visitors. But you will remember it for an-other reason. In the cathedral, whose towers soar above the narrow streets, there is a magnificent mosaic of Christ-in-Majesty—a simple, moving, dramatic 12th-century representation of the spirit of faith. The cloister, with its twisted columns and pointed arches, is no less interest-ing.

Messina. At the northeast corner of the island closest to the mainland, Messina is a city of legend and disaster. It was founded in the 8th century B.C. and as an ally of Rome was one of the instigators of the Punic wars with Carthage. In 1908 it was all but obliterated by one of the most destructive earthquakes of modern times, a disaster which in a few moments took the lives of 60,000 people, more than half the population of the town. The modern city, completely rebuilt at that time (and rebuilt again after the bombings of World War II) is a model of design and planning, one of the handsomest and busiest cities in Italy. Its bathing beach, the ultra-modern *Lido Mortelle,* is among the best on the island, known especially for its fine, white sand.

Taormina. Taormina is frankly a resort and it has been enchanting tourists ever since it was founded as a Greek colony in the 4th century B.C. Few places can match its natural beauty. Like a vast terrace it clings to a sheer mountainside some 700 feet above the Mediterranean, looking out over the luminous blue water below—you will see the lights of the spear fishermen's boats bobbing all night—and to the south to majestic Mount Etna, only a few miles away. Equipped with excellent restaurants and hotels (chief of them being the famed Hotel San Domenico, a former monastery which boasts one of the most beautiful gardens in Italy), and with good beaches nearby, Taormina is some-thing of a vacationist's year-round paradise. It also has its full share of classic and medieval remains, notably the fine Greek theater with flower-overgrown stone seats that look out past the crumbled stage to the smoking white peak of Etna.

Catania. Halfway down the eastern coast and near the base of Mount Etna is Catania, Sicily's second largest city. It is of ancient origin, but it has so often been destroyed by volcanic eruptions and earthquakes that little remains of its history in antiquity. It looks like what it now is—a flourishing commercial and tourist center with handsome wide streets, spacious squares, and some fine 18th-century buildings.

Mount Etna. The largest active volcano in Europe, Etna dominates the whole eastern shore of Sicily. An excellent new road carries you well up past the timber line, and a modern cable car has replaced the donkeys that used to carry the more energetic tourists up to the crater. The snow fields, covered for six months of the year on the upper slopes, have made Etna a popular and well-developed winter sports area.

Syracuse (Siracusa). A lively city with a handsome wide port. Syracuse is hardly the metropolis it was when Cicero described it as "the largest of the Greek cities and the most beautiful in the world." But beautiful it still is and much remains, too, of the ancient city. The splendidly situated theater that Dionysius built twenty-three centuries ago still stands in excellent condition—and still is used for the elaborate productions of classic Greek dramas given there every spring. There is also a huge but less perfectly preserved Roman amphitheater. Most curious are the chasms, or open caverns in the rocks, called *latomie.* They are now beautiful sunken gardens, but they were once used as prisons. Thousands of captured Athenian soldiers were on one occasion thrown into these gorges and left to starve. The most famous of the latomie is called the *Ear of Dionysius* because of its amazing acoustics which, it is said, made it possible for the tyrant listening above to catch the slightest whisper among the prisoners below.

On the outskirts of Syracuse are the burial sites of the Siculi, the early inhabitants of prehistoric Sicily, in huge cliffs pitted with hewn-out caverns. And nearby, in the Achradina section, are the Christian catacombs—the largest in the world, far surpassing those in Rome.

The approach to Taormina   *Columns of the temple at Segesta*

Agrigento. The Greek remains in Agrigento are the finest on the island and among the best in the world. In the *Valley of the Temples* stand half a dozen magnificent Doric structures that are certainly without peers except in Greece itself—and there are authorities who rate these splendidly preserved buildings as superior to all but one or two of the temples in Greece. They are mainly from the 6th and 5th centuries B.C. and they stand magnificently apart from the modern city which has grown up on the hill above. With their gold and amber color showing handsomely against the hills or (in spring) against the almond blossoms in the plains below, they are an experience in time and beauty that no one forgets. Noblest of all is the *Temple of Concordia,* with all of its 34 columns intact, a work of art that is one of the best preserved Greek temples in the world, second only to the Temple of Theseus in Athens.

Selinunte. Once the illustrious city of Selinus, Selinunte has the most gigantic Greek remains on the island, dating from the 7th to the 3rd century B.C. when the city was one of the most powerful and progressive centers of Sicilian civilization. Pillaged by Carthage in 409 A.D. and later ruined, it is thought, by an earthquake, the temples are now an immense expanse of scattered ruins. Among the most famous of them (they are still designated by letters rather than by name) the most striking are the colossal "G" (550 B.C.) and the archaic "C" whose marvelous metope is displayed in the Palermo Museum. Temple "G" must have been one of the most immense Greek structures in the world. The stone blocks that form the bottom segments of the columns weigh a hundred tons and measure up to 11 feet in diameter.

Segesta. Segesta was the great rival of Selinus in ancient days, but when it fell to the Vandals and Saracens they laid it waste. All that remains today is one vast antique theater and a single Doric temple from the 5th century B.C. But this one great building, standing majestically alone

The magnificent Temple of Concordia at Agrigento

in the austere hills, has for some people a beauty that exceeds even that at Agrigento.

The western tip of the island also has much to offer. There is *Erice,* a beautiful medieval town set on a promontory between the bay and the open sea. And *Marsala,* the ancient Carthagenian city best known today for the rich wine that bears its name.

But if you are pressed for time, an hour's drive northeast will bring you within sight of the cluster of domes and towers silhouetted above Monte Pellegrino. You are at Palermo, the end—and the beginning— of your circuit of Sicily.

SARDINIA

Next to Sicily the largest of the Italian islands, Sardinia (Sardegna) is no longer off the beaten track. Until fairly recently, Sardinia remained relatively primitive, rugged and wild, but a considerable number of very good and unusual hotels have been developed over the past few years, and the island has become Italy's newest important tourist attraction. The trip is not difficult—overnight by steamer from Civitavecchia or less than one hour by plane from Rome—and the island has a completely unspoiled charm that will appeal to many. Its mountain-and-sea beauty (there are excellent beaches both in the north and south), its handsome swarthy people, its rich and interesting folklore and customs, the colorful costumes and fiestas—all will delight the visitor. But the main attraction is perhaps the island scenery itself— the mountains, the villages, the strange prehistoric stone defense works called *nuraghe,* the caves and grottos that dot the hills, the beautiful orange and lemon groves.

There are a number of sizeable towns to see. **Cagliari,** the main port of entry, is the capital and principal city. It has an excellent museum in which the history of the island is vividly recreated, and a fine 14th-century cathedral with much Sardinian decoration and a superb picture gallery. There is also the fortress with its two fine towers and a view that is spectacular.

Sassari, at the northern end, is the second most important city. Its museum, specializing in regional art is worth a visit, as is the 12th-century Romanesque church, *Santissima Trinità di Saccargia,* just outside the city. The most expensive and exclusive summer resort in Italy is on Sardinia's northeast coast. Developed by the Aga Khan and known as the **Emerald Coast** (Costa Smevalda), it is a complex of small hotels and villas nestled on the slopes above emerald bays. The keynote is simplicity, even though the yachts anchored in the harbor can very nearly compete with ocean liners. Film stars and jet-setters and European nobility are so much in evidence that they cause no stir.

CHAPTER *6*

ITALIAN

We have all heard stories about tourists who have traveled through Italy knowing only two Italian words—*scusi* and *prego*—and they say they got along famously. Others claim that all you really need to know are *quanto?* (how much?) and its logical sequence—*troppo!* (too much!).

However, there are occasions when a few words might have helped them out of a tight spot. Nothing flatters the people of a country more than knowing a foreigner has made the attempt to learn a few words and phrases of his language. The traveler who in some small way breaks down the language barrier can turn a difficult situation into an adventure. A feeling of warmth is created immediately between two people from different parts of the world who can exchange a few words—however halting and mispronounced they may be.

PRONUNCIATION

If you follow a few simple rules, Italian pronunciation is not difficult. The *a* is pronounced as in fäther; *i* as in fēēd; *u* as in fōōd; *e* as in lĕt or as in thēy; *o* as in lōw or as in broth. Consonants are pronounced approximately as they are in English except for the *c* which follows these rules: *c* or *cc* before e or i is pronounced *ch;* *c* or *cc* before h, a, o, u is pronounced *k.*

General Phrases

Please}	*per piacere*	pehr pyah-che h-reh
	per favore	pehr fah-vo h-reh
Thank you	*grazie*	gra h-tsyeh
Thank you very much	*grazie mille*	gra h-tsyeh mee l-leh
Excuse me	*Scusi*	skoo-see

The slopes of Mt. Etna, a popular winter playground

Good morning	*Buon giorno*	bwawn johr-noh
Good evening	*Buona sera*	bwaw-nah seh-rah
Good night	*Buona notte*	bwaw-nah nawt-teh
Hello (on telephone only)	*Pronto!*	prohn-toh
	Ciao	chah-oh
Goodbye}	*Arrivederci*	ahr-ree-veh-dehr-chee
How are you?	*Come sta?*	koh-meh stah?
I am well, thank you	*Bene, grazie*	beh-neh grah-tsyeh
I do not understand	*Non capisco*	nohn kah-pees-koh
Come in (in answer to knock on door)	*Avanti!*	ah-vahn-tee
How does one say	*Come is dice*	koh-meh see dee-cheh
All right	*Va bene*	vah beh-neh
How much is it?	*Quanto costa?*	kwahn-toh koh-stah
It is too expensive	*Costa troppo*	koh-stah trawp-poh
I am sorry	*Mi dispiace*	mee dees-pyah-cheh
Yes (No) sir, madam, miss	*Si (No) signore, signora, signorina*	see (naw) see-nyoh-reh, see-nyoh-rah, see-nyoh-ree-nah
What time is it?	*Che ora è?*	kay oh-rah eh?
Where is the ladies' room?	*Dov'è il gabinetto per signore?*	dohv-eh eel gah-bee-neht-toh pehr see-nyoh-reh?
I feel sick	*Mi sento male*	mee sehn-toh mah-leh
I need a doctor	*Ho bisogno di un medico*	aw bee-zaw-nyoh dee oon meh-dee-koh
Where is—?	*Dov'è—?*	dohv-eh—?
Bring me—	*Mi porti—*	mee pawr-tee—
Speak slowly	*Parli lentamente*	pahr-lee lehn-tah-mehn-teh

At the Hotel

I would like a single (double) room with (without) bath.
Vorrei una camera per uno (due) con (senza) bagno.
Voh-rehee oo-nah kah-meh-rah pehr oo-noh (doo-eh) kohn (sehn-tsah) bah-nyoh.

How much is it per day?
Quanto costa al giorno?
Kwahn-toh kohs-tah ahl johr-noh?
Does that include service and taxes?
È tutto compreso—servizio e tasse?
Eh toot-toh kohm-preh-soh sehr-vee-tsyoh eh tahs-seh?

May I see the room?
Posso vedere la camera?
Paws-soh veh-deh-reh lah kah-meh-rah?

Is there a restaurant (garage)?
C'è il ristorante (garage)?
Cheh eel rees-toh-rahn-teh (gah-rahy)?

Please call me at seven o'clock in the morning.
Per favore mi chiami alle sette di mattina.
Pehr fah-voh-reh mee kyah-mee ahl-leh seht-teh dee maht-tee-nah.

I would like to order breakfast.
Vorrei ordinare la prima colazione.
Vohr-rehee ohr-dee-nah-reh lah pree-mah coh-lah-tsyoh-neh.

I would like to make a telephone call.
Vorrei fare una telefonata.
Vohr-reh-ee fah-reh oo-nah teh-leh-foh-nah-tah.

Bring me more blankets (hangers).
Mi porti più coperte (attaccapanni).
Mee pawr-tee pyoo koh-pehr-teh (aht-tahk-kah-pahn-nee).

At what time is dinner served?
A che ora è servito il pranzo?
Ah keh oh-rah eh sehr-vee-toh eel prahn-dsoh?

Is there any mail for me?
C'è posta per me?
Cheh paws-tah pehr meh?

I would like to have some laundry done.
Vorrei fare lavare la biancheria,
Vohr-reh-ee fah-reh lah-vah-reh lah bee-ahn-keh-ree-ah.

I shall leave tomorrow morning.
Partirò domani mattina.
Pahr-tee-roh doh-mah-nee maht-tee-nah.

In the Restaurant
Waiter, the menu, please.
Cameriere, la lista, per favore.
Kah-mehr-yeh-reh, lah lees-tah, pehr fah-voh-reh.

I would like a bottle of mineral water.
Vorrei una bottiglia d'acqua minerale.
Vohr-reh-ee oo-nah boht-tee-lyah dahk-kwah mee-neh-rah-leh.

I would like a half bottle of red table wine.
Vorrei una mezza bottiglia di vino da tavola rosso.
Vohr-reh-ee oo-na meh-dzah boht-tee-lyah dee vee-noh dah tah-voh-lah rohs-soh.

I need a fork.
Ho bisogno di una forchetta.
Aw bee-zaw-nyoh dee oo-nah fohr-keht-tah.

I would like some ice in the water.
Vorrei del ghiaccio nell' acqua.
Vohr-reh-ee dehl gyah-choh nehl ahk-kwah.

Please bring me some more butter.
Mi porti un altro po'di burro, per favore.
Mee pawr-tee oon ahl-troh paw dee boor-roh, pehr fah-voh-reh.

Bring me a broiled steak—rare.
Mi porti una bistecca ai ferri al sangue.
Mee pawr-tee *oo*-na bee-stehk-kah ahee fehr-ree ahl *sahn*-gway.

Bring us some caffè expresso.
Ci porti del caffè espresso.
Chee pawr-tee dehl kahf-feh ehs-prehs-soh.

On the Road
Is this the road to Rome?
È questa la strada per andare a Roma?
Eh kwehs-tah lah strah-dah pehr ahn-dah-reh ah Roh-mah?

Do I go straight ahead or turn right (left)?
Devo andare diritto o voltare a destra (a sinistra)?
Deh-voh ahn-dah-reh dee-reet-toh oh vohl-tah-reh ah dehs-strah (ah see-nees-trah)?

Please fill my tank.
Riempia il serbatoio, per favore.
Ree-*ehm*-pyah eel sehr-bah-toh-yoh, pehr fah-voh-reh.

Here is my driver's license.
Ecco la mia patente di circolazione.
*Eh*k-koh lah mee-ah pah-*teh*n-teh dee cheer-koh-lah-ts*yo*h-neh.

The car won't start.
Il motore non vuole partire.
Eel moh-*toh*-reh nawn vw*aw*-leh pahr-*tee*-reh.

How far is Rome?
A quanta distanza si trova Roma?
Ah kw*ah*n-tah dees-*tah*n-tsah see tr*oh*-vah Roh-mah?

Is there a gas station near here?
C'è una stazione di rifornimento* qui vicino?
Cheh *oo*-na stah-tsy*oh*-neh dee ree-for-nee-*meh*n-toh kwee vee-chee-noh?
*also: *pompa di benzina*—p*oh*m-pah dee behn-dz*ee*-nah

Train or Bus Travel
I would like two first class tickets to Milan.
Vorrei due biglietti di prima classe per Milano.
Vohr-r*eh*-ee doo-eh bee-ly*eh*t-tee dee pree-mah kl*ah*s-seh pehr mee-l*ah*-noh.

How much is a round trip ticket? (one way only)
Quanto costa un biglietto di andata e ritorno? (solo andata)
Kw*ah*n-toh k*oh*-stah oon bee-ly*e*ht-toh dee ahn-*dah*-tah eh ree-*toh*r-noh? (soh-loh ahn-dah-tah)

Is there a dining car (pullman) on this train?
C'è il vagone ristorante (letti) su questo treno?
Cheh eel vah-*goh*-neh rees-toh-r*ah*n-teh (l*e*ht-tee) soo kw*e*hs-toh tr*eh*-noh?

At what time does the train (bus) leave for Rome?
A che ora parte il treno (l'autobus) per Roma?
Ah kay *o*h-rah p*ah*r-teh eel tr*eh*-noh (l*ah*oo-toh-boos) pehr r*oh*-mah?

Where is the ticket office?
Dov'è la biglietteria?
Doh-ve h lah bee-lyet-teh-*ree*-ah?

From which track does the train leave?
Da quale binario parte il treno?
Dah kw*ah*-leh bee-n*ah*-ryoh p*ah*r-teh eel tr*eh*-noh?

I have lost a valise.
Ho perduto una valigia.
Aw pehr-d*oo*-toh *oo*-nah vah-*lee*-ja.

I would like to leave this baggage here.
Vorrei lasciare questi bagagli qui.
Vohr-*reh*-ee lah-sh*ah*-reh kw*eh*s-tee bah-g*ah*-lyee kwee.

Signs

Signore	Ladies	*A destra*	To the right
Donne	Women	*A sinistra*	To the left
Signori	Gentlemen	*Velocita massima*	Speed limit
Uomini	Men	*Procedere con*	Caution
Vietato fumare	No smoking	*prudenza*	
Vietato il	No parking	*Passaggio a*	Railroad
parcheggio		*livello*	crossing
Senso unico	One way street	*Fili ad alta*	High tension
Entrata	Entrance	*tensione*	wires
Uscita	Exit	*Alt*	Stop (halt)

VOCABULARY

Colors

black	*nero*	neh-roh
blue	*azzurro*	ah-dz*oo*r-roh
brown	*marrone*	mah-r*oh*-neh

green	*verde*	veh r-deh
red	*rosso*	roh s-soh
white	*bianco*	bee-*yah* n-koh
yellow	*giallo*	jee-*ah* l-loh

Numbers:

1.	*uno*	*oo*-no	18.	*diciotto*	dee-ch*ot*-toh
2.	*due*	d*oo*-eh	19.	*diciannove*	dee-chahn-n*aw*-ve
3.	*tre*	treh	20.	*venti*	veh n-tee
4.	*quattro*	kw*ah*t-troh	21.	*ventuno*	vehn-*too*-noh
5.	*cinque*	chee n-kweh	22.	*ventidue*	vehn-tee-d*oo*-eh
6.	*sei*	say	23.	*ventitre*	vehn-tee-tr*eh*
7.	*sette*	s*eh*t-teh	28.	*ventotto*	vehn-t*aw*t-toh
8.	*otto*	*aw*t-toh	30.	*trenta*	tr*eh* n-tah
9.	*nove*	n*aw*-veh	40.	*quaranta*	kwah-r*ah* n-tah
10.	*dieci*	dee*ye*h-chee	50.	*cinquanta*	cheen-kw*an*-tah
11.	*undici*	*oo* n-dee-chee	60.	*sessanta*	sehs-s*ah* n-tah
12.	*dodici*	d*oh*-dee-chee	70.	*settanta*	seht-t*ah* n-tah
13.	*tredici*	tr*eh*-dee-chee	80.	*ottanta*	awt-t*ah* n-tah
14.	*quattordici*	kw*ah*t-tohr-dee-chee	90.	*novanta*	naw-v*ah* n-tah
15.	*quindici*	kw*ee* n-dee-chee	100.	*cento*	ch*eh* n-toh
16.	*sedici*	s*eh*-dee-chee	200.	*duecento*	doo-eh-chen-toh
17.	*diciassette*	dee-chahs-s*eh* t-teh	500.	*cinquecento*	cheen-kweh-ch*eh* n-to
			1000.	*mille*	mee l-leh

Days of the Week:

Monday	*lunedi*	loo-neh-d*ee*
Tuesday	*martedi*	mahr-teh-d*ee*
Wednesday	*mercoledi*	mehr-caw-leh-d*ee*
Thursday	*giovedi*	joh-veh-d*ee*
Friday	*venerdi*	veh-nehr-d*ee*
Saturday	*sabato*	s*ah*-bah-toh
Sunday	*domenica*	doh-m*eh*-nee-kah

Months

January	*gennaio*	jehn-n*ah*-yoh
February	*febbraio*	fehb-br*ah*-yoh
March	*marzo*	m*ah*r-tsoh
April	*aprile*	ah-pr*ee*-leh
May	*maggio*	m*a*h-joh
June	*giugno*	jee-y*oo*-nyoh
July	*luglio*	l*oo*-lyoh
August	*agosto*	ah-g*oh*s-toh
September	*settembre*	seht-t*eh*m-breh
October	*ottobre*	awt-t*oh*-breh
November	*novembre*	naw-v*eh*m-breh
December	*dicembre*	dee-ch*eh*m-bre

General

after	*dopo*	d*oh*-poh
afternoon	*il pomeriggio*	eel poh-meh-r*ee*-joh
air	*l'aria*	l*ah*r yah
airplane	*l'aereo*	lah-*eh*-reh-oh
all	*tutto*	t*oo*t-toh
aspirin	*l'aspirina*	lahs-peh-r*ee*-nah
automobile	*l'automobile, la macchina*	l ahoo-toh-m*oh*-bee-leh lah m*ah*-kee-nah
bad	*cattivo*	cah-t*ee*-voh
bank	*la banca*	lah b*ah*n-kah
barber	*il barbiere*	eel bahr-b*ye*h-reh
bath room	*la stanza da bagno*	lah st*ah*n-tsah dah b*ah*-nyoh
beautiful	*bello*	b*eh*l-loh
beauty parlor	*parrucchiere*	pahr-roo-kee-*eh*-rah
bedroom	*la camera da letto*	lah c*ah*-meh-rah dah l*eh*t-toh
beef	*il manzo*	eel m*ah*n-dzoh
beer	*la birra*	lah b*ee*r-rah
bill	*il conto*	eel k*oh*n-toh
boat	*la nave—il vapore*	lah n*ah*-veh or eel vah-p*oh*-re
bottle	*la bottiglia*	lah boht-t*ee*-lyah
box	*la scatola*	lah sk*ah*-toh-lah
boy	*il ragazzo*	eel rah-g*ah*-tsoh
brakes	*i freni*	ee fr*eh*-nee
bread	*il pane*	eel p*ah*-neh
breakfast	*la prima colazione*	la pree-ma coh-lawtsy-*oh*-neh

bring	*portare*	pohr-t*ah*-reh
broken	*guasto*	*gwas*-toh
bus	*l'autobus*	lah*oo*-to-boos
bus stop	*fermata*	fehr-m*ah*-tah
butter	*il burro*	eel b*oo*r-roh
buy	*comprare*	kohm-pr*ah*-re
carburetor	*il carburatore*	eel kahr-boo-rah-t*oh*-reh
cashier	*il cassiere*	eel kahs-sy*e*h-reh
cathedral	*la cattedrale, il duomo*	lah kaht-teh-dr*ah*-leh, or eel dw*aw*-moh
cheap	*economico*	eh-kohn-ee-*mee*-koh
check (bank)	*l'assegno*	lahs-s*e*h-nyoh
cheese	*il formaggio*	eel fohr-m*ah*-joh
chicken	*il pollo*	eel p*oh*l-loh
church	*la chiesa*	lah kee-*yeh*-zah
clothes	*i vestiti*	ee ves-*tee*-tee
coffee	*il caffè*	eel kahf-f*e*h
cold	*freddo*	fr*eh*d-doh
come	*venire*	veh-n*ee*-reh
compartment (train)	*lo scompartimento*	loh skohm-pahr-tee-m*eh*n-toh
conductor	*il controllore*	eel kohn-trohl-l*oh*-reh
cost (v.)	*costare*	kohs-t*ah*-reh
cotton	*il cotone*	eel koh-t*oh*-neh
cup	*la tazza*	lah t*ah*-tsah
dark	*scuro*	sk*oo*-roh
day	*il giorno*	eel j*oh*r-noh
dentist	*il dentista*	eel dehn-t*ee*s-tah
depart	*partire*	pahr-t*ee*-reh
dessert	*dolce*	d*oh*l-cheh
difficult	*difficile*	deef-*fee*-chee-leh
dining room	*la sala da pranzo*	lah s*ah*-lah da pr*ah*n-dsoh
dining car	*il vagone ristorante*	eel vah-*goh*-neh rees-toh-r*ah*n-teh
dinner	*il pranzo*	eel pr*ah*n-dsoh
doctor	*il medico*	eel m*eh*-dee-coh
door	*la porta*	lah p*oh*r-tah
dress	*il vestito*	eel vehs-*tee*-toh
drink (v.)	*bere*	b*eh*-reh
drug store	*la farmacia*	lah fahr-mah-ch*ee*-ah
dry clean	*lavare a secco*	lah-v*ah*-reh ah s*eh*k-koh
east	*est*	ehst
easy	*facile*	fah-chee-leh
eat	*mangiare*	mahn-j*ah*-reh
egg	*l'uovo*	l'w*aw*-voh
engine (auto)	*il motore*	eel moh-t*oh*-reh
evening	*la sera*	lah s*eh*-rah
expensive	*caro*	c*ah*-roh
far	*lontano*	lohn-t*ah*-noh
ferry boat	*traghetto*	trah-g*et*-toh

find	trovare	troh-vah-reh
fish	il pesce	eel peh-sheh
floor (story)	il piano	eel pyah-noh
fork	la forchetta	lah fohr-keht-tah
gasoline	la benzina	lah behndzee-nah
girl	la ragazza	lah rah-gah-tsah
glass (drinking)	il bicchiere	eel beek-kyeh-reh
gloves	i guanti	ee gwahn-tee
good	buono	bwaw-noh
guide	la guida	lah gwee-dah
half (adj.)	mezzo	meh-dzoh
ham	il prosciutto	eel proh-shoot-toh
handbag	la borsetta	lah bohr-seht-tah
handkerchief	il fazzoletto	eel fah-dzoh-leht-toh
hat	il cappello	eel kahp-pehl-loh
heat	il calore	eel kah-loh-reh
hospital	l'ospedale	lohs-peh-dah-leh
hot	caldo	kahl-doh
husband	il marito	eel mah-ree-toh
ice	il ghiaccio	eel gyah-choh
ill	malato	mah-lah-toh
key	la chiave	lah kyah-veh
knife	il coltello	eel cohl-tehl-loh
know (a fact, how to)	sapere	sah-peh-reh
know (acquainted with)	conoscere	coh-noh-sheh-reh
large	grande	grahn-deh
laundress	la lavandaia	lah lah-vahn-dah-yah
lavatory (W.C.)	il gabinetto	eel gah-bee-neht-toh
left	sinistra	see-nees-trah
less	meno	meh-noh
long	lungo	loon-goh
lose (v.)	perdere	pehr-deh-reh
lunch	la colazione	lah koh-lah-tsyoh-neh
maid	la cameriera	lah kah-mehr-yeh-rah
man	l'uomo	l'waw-moh
manager	il direttore	eel dee-reht-toh-reh
map (road)	la carta (stradale)	lah cahr-tah (strah-dah-leh)
meal	il pasto	eel pahs-toh
meat	la carne	lah cahr-neh
mechanic	il meccanico	eel mehk-kah-nee-koh
menu	la lista	lah lees-tah
milk	il latte	eel laht-teh
mistake	lo sbaglio	loh zbah-lyoh
more	più	p'yoo
morning	la mattina	lah maht-tee-nah
museum	il museo	eel moo-zeh-oh
name	il nome	eel noh-meh
napkin	il tovagliolo	eel toh-vah-lyoh-loh
near	vicino	vee-chee-noh
night	la notte	lah nawt-teh
north	nord	nawrd

now	*adesso*	ah-*deh*s-soh
ship	*nave*	*nah*-veh
south	*sud*	sood
spoon	*il cucchiaio*	eel kook-ky*ah*-yo
stamp	*il francobollo*	eel frahn-koh b*oh*l-loh
station	*la stazione*	lah stah-tsy*oh*-neh
steak	*la bistecca*	lah bees-*teh*k-kah
stockings	*le calze*	leh *kah*l-tseh
store, shop	*il negozio*	eel neh-g*oh*-tsyoh
suit	*l'abito*	*lah*-bee-toh
supper	*la cena*	lah ch*eh*-nah
sweater	*la maglia*	lah m*ah*-lyah
sweet	*dolce*	d*oh*l-cheh
tailor	*il sarto*	eel s*ah*r-toh
taxi	*il tassí*	eel tahs-s*ee*
tea	*il tè*	eel teh
teaspoon	*il cucchiaino*	eel kook-kyah-*ee*-noh
telephone	*il telefono*	eel teh-l*eh*-foh-noh
theater	*il teatro*	eel teh-*ah*-troh
ticket	*il biglietto*	eel bee-ly*eh*t-toh
timetable	*l'orario*	law-r*ah*-ryoh
tip	*la mancia*	lah m*ah*n-chah
tire (auto)	*la gomma*	lah g*oh*m-mah
today	*oggi*	*oh*-jee
tomorrow	*domani*	doh-m*ah*-nee
tonight	*stasera*	stah-s*eh*-rah
towel	*l'asciugamano*	lah-shoo-gah-m*ah*-noh
track	*il binario*	eel bee-n*ah*-ryoh
train	*il treno*	eel tr*eh*-noh
trip	*il viaggio*	eel vee-*ah*-joh
trousers	*i pantaloni, calzoni*	ee pahn-tah-l*oh*-nee, ee cahl-ts*oh*-nee
use (verb)	*usare*	oo-z*ah*-reh
valise	*la valigia*	lah vah-l*ee*-jah
veal	*il vitello*	eel vee-t*eh*l-loh
wait	*aspettare*	ahs-peht-t*ah*-reh
wallet	*il portafoglio*	eel pohr-tah-f*oh*-lyoh
wash	*lavare*	lah-v*ah*-reh
water (mineral)	*l'acqua (minerale)*	*lah*k-kwah (mee-neh-*rah*-leh)
west	*ovest*	*oh*-vehst
when	*quando*	kw*ah*n-doh
where	*dove*	d*oh*-veh
who	*chi*	kee
why	*perchè*	pehr-k*eh*
wife	*la moglie*	lah m*oh*-lyeh
window	*la finestra*	lah fee-n*eh*s-trah
wine	*il vino*	eel v*ee*-noh
with	*con*	kohn
without	*senza*	s*eh*n-tsah
woman	*la donna*	lah d*oh*n-nah
yesterday	*ieri*	y*eh*-ree

CHAPTER 7

FACT FINDER

This section is basically a brief guide to a selected list of hotels and restaurants in the more important tourist centers of Italy. Other helpful information, such as *Best Buys* and *Useful Addresses,* is given for the larger cities.

The hotels listed here have been divided into four groups, which correspond roughly to the official categories established by ENIT, the government tourist bureau. The symbol preceding the name of the hotel indicates the class to which it belongs: ****De Luxe; ***First Class; **Medium Priced; and *Inexpensive. For more information about hotels and their classifications, see Chapter 3, WHAT YOU SHOULD KNOW ABOUT ITALY.

In a brief guide of this kind it is impossible to list rates exactly. All hotels have, of course, a considerable range of prices for any particular type of accommodation. Rates are usually a bit lower in smaller towns than in large cities. In some areas, in addition, there is one established rate for the high season, and a lower one for the off-season period. In general, expect that during the busy tourist season most hotels will ask the maximum permissible rate or something close to it.

The table below will give you a reasonably accurate idea of the minimum and maximum rates at the time of publication. For De Luxe and First Class hotels, the prices quoted generally cover everything, including the tax (which for reasons perhaps not even known to the Italians can sometimes be slightly higher than the usual 18%), service, and breakfast. In Moderate Priced and Inexpensive hotels, the price quoted here (and by the hotels themselves) is more likely to represent a base rate, with tax, service, etc., added on separately. In some hotels there is an additional charge for air-conditioning or heating, varying

Convent of Palma di Montechiaro in Sicily

from 4,000 lire to perhaps 6,000 lire ($2.85 to $4.28). The exchange rate for the lira is figured at 1,400 to the dollar. Because exchange rates fluctuate so, it would be a good idea to check the latest rates with Italian Government Tourist Office or your travel agent before you start out.

Single with bath	Double with bath	Single without bath	Single with bath
De Luxe			
175,000	270,000	None	None
320,000 l.–$228	440,000 l.–$315		
First Class			
70,000 l.	135,000 l.	None	None
200,000 l.–$142	270,000 l.–$193		
Moderate			
35,000 l.	65,000 l.	30,000 l.	50,000 l.
90,000 l.–$64	130,000 l.–$93	65,000 l.–$46	110,000 l.–$79
Inexpensive			
20,000 l.	45,000 l.	20,000	35,000 l.
35,000 l.–$25	59,000 l.–$42	27,000–$19	44,000 l.–$32

NOTE: Prices are somewhat higher in Milan and Venice.

It is even more difficult to characterize restaurants accurately and helpfully than it is to classify hotels. The problem always involves a complicated mixture of such matters as price, preference, and personal taste. In the listing that follows, however, symbols have been used to indicate three general *types* of eating places: ***fine, de luxe restaurants; **excellent restaurants in the middle range; *more modest places with good, well-prepared food.

Within broad limitations, prices are what you make them. Dinner in a fashionable luxury restaurant will usually cost in the neighborhood of 40,000 lire ($28.50) per person, not including beverages, cover and service. These will probably add another 40 per cent to your bill. Needless to say, you can go well above these figures if you try, particularly in cities like Rome, Milan and Florence. The prices in provincial cities are correspondingly less. In a medium priced restaurant about 20,000 lire ($14.25) before extras. But in a *trattoria,* a smaller place with more modest decor, you can have a wholesome, substantial meal from 10,000 to 15,000 lire ($7.15 to $10.70).

Agrigento (Sicily) (pop. 51,000)

HOTELS: ***Villa Athena,* Località i Templi. 41 rooms. ***Jolly dei Templi,* Parco Angeli-Villaggio Mose. 146 rooms. ***Dei Pini,* Località Vincenzella, Porto Empedocle. 138 rooms. ***Della-Valle,* Via dei Templi. 88 rooms. Air-conditioned.

RESTAURANTS: ***Del Vigneto,* Via Cavalieri magazzeni, 11. Scenic with terrace. **Panorama,* Via F. Crispi 2.

Alghero (Sardinia) (pop. 38,000)

HOTELS: ***Calabona,* Calabona. 113 rooms. ***Las Tronas,* Lungomare Valencia 1. 31 rooms. * *Eleonora,* Viale Valencia. 71 rooms. Sea, pool, garages. ***La Margherita,* 65 rooms.

RESTAURANTS: ***La Lepanto.* Via C. Alberto 125. **Dieci Metri,* Vicolo Adami 47.

Amalfi (pop. 6,100)

HOTELS: ***Cappuccini,* 43 rooms (another 16 in annex). Medieval convent made into a hotel, on cliff overlooking Bay of Amalfi. ***Luna.* 42 rooms. ***Il Saraceno.* 56 rooms. ****Santa Caterina,* on route 163, 1 km. W. of Amalfi. 75 rooms with three annexes. Garden and view of sea. ***Miramalfi,* on route 163, 1 km. W. of Amalfi. 43 rooms. **Marina Riviera.* 20 rooms. Open April to Oct.

RESTAURANTS: ***Cappuccini.* Garden, sea view, dancing. ***Santa Caterina,* on Route 163, 1 km. W. of Amalfi. Terrace, garden, sea view. ** *La Marinella,* Lungomare dei Cavalieri. Dancing, private beach.

Ancona (pop. 105,600)

HOTELS: ***Jolly,* Rupi di Via XXIX Settembre 14. 88 rooms. New, comfortable. ***Grand Hotel Palace,* Lungomare Vanvitelli 24 (Sea Drive). 40 rooms. Air-conditioned. ***Pass-etto,* 1 Via Thaon di Revel. 45 rooms. View, garden. **Motel AGIP,* S.S. 16 Adriatica, 51 rooms.

RESTAURANTS: ***Moretta,* Via Matteotti 81. **I Glicini,* Via Montagnola 25, outside town. Regional food.

Arezzo (pop. 92,000)

HOTEL: ***Continentale,* 7 Piazza Guido Monaco. 80 rooms.

RESTAURANT: **Buca di San Francesco,* 1 Piazza San Francesco. 13th-century atmosphere.

Assisi (pop. 26,000)

HOTELS: ***Giotto,* 41 Via Fonte Bella. 69 rooms. ***Subasio,* Frate Elia 2. 75 rooms.

RESTAURANT: ***Taverna d'Arco,* 8 Via S. Gregorio.

Bari (pop. 387,000)

HOTELS: ***Palace,* 13 Via Lombardi. 210 rooms. ***Jolly,* Via G. Petroni 15. 164 rooms. ***Boston,* Via Piccinni 155. 72 rooms. Air-conditioned, garage. ***Victor,* Via Nicolai 71. 75 rooms. **Adria,* 10 Via Luigi Zuppetta. 38 rooms.

RESTAURANTS: ***Sorso Preferito,* Via De Nicolo, 46 ***La Pignata,* Via Melo 9.

Bergamo (pop. 128,000)

HOTELS: ***Agnello d'oro,* Via Gombito 22. 25 rooms. ***Excelsior San Marco,* 6 Piazzale della Republica. 151 rooms. **Del Moro,* Largo Porta Nuova 6. 25 rooms. Air-conditioned.

RESTAURANTS: ***Tino Fontana,* Pz. Repubblica 6. Original dishes. ***Manarini,* 5 Viale Vittorio Emanuele. ***Del Moro,* Largo Porta Nuova 6. ***Dell'Angelo,* Via S. Caterina 55.

Bologna (pop. 448,000)

HOTELS: ***Internazionale,* Via dell'Indipendenza 60. 139 rooms. ***

Jolly, 2 Piazza XX Settembre. 172 rooms. ***Milano-Excelsior,* 51 Via Pietramellara. 78 rooms. ***Roma,* 9 Via D'Azeglio. 87 rooms. ***Alexander,* Via Pietramellara 47. 108 rooms.

RESTAURANTS: ****Al Pappagallo,* 3 Piazza Mercanzia. ****Cantunzein,* 4 Piazza Verdi. ***Diana,* 24 Via Indipendenza. ****Tre Galli d'Oro,* 42 Via Stalingrado. ***Grada,* Via della Grada 6. Very good pasta. ***Cesarina,* 19 Via Santo Stefano. ***Nerina,* 6 Piazza Galileo. ***Rodrigo,* Via della Zecca 2/H. **San Martino,* Piazza San Martino 9. **Serghei,* Via Piella 12, Small family-style trattoria.

ADDRESSES: *Ente Provinciale per il Turismo,* Via Marconi 45 and railway station. *CIT,* 2 Piazza Nettuno. *Automobile Club,* Via Baracca 2.

Bolzano (pop. 106,000)

HOTELS: ****Park Laurin,* 4 Via Laurin. 120 rooms. Garden with swimming pool, tennis courts. ***Alpi,* 35 Via Alto Adige. 116 rooms. ****Grifone,* 7 Piazza Walter. 140 rooms. Swimming pool, tennis. ***Eurotel Sciliar,* Alpe di Siusi. 84 rooms. **Motel Kampill,* Via Campiglio 11. 25 rooms.

RESTAURANTS: ***Da Abramo,* Pz. Gries 16. ***Chez frederic,* 12 Armando Diaz. **Moritzingerhof,* Via Merano, 113.

Brescia (pop. 204,000)

HOTELS: ****Ambasciatori,* Via Crocifissa, 92, 66 rooms. ***Master,* Via Apollonio 72. 76 rooms.

RESTAURANTS: ****La Sosta,* 20 Via S. Martino della Battaglia. ***La Buta,* Via Groppallo, 23. Good food in lovely building with courtyard.

Cagliari (Sardinia) (pop. 241,000)

HOTELS: ****Castello,* Cagliari. 142 rooms. ***Panorama,* Vle. A. Diaz,

231, 97 rooms. ***Mediterraneo,* Lungomare C. Colombo 46. 140 rooms. **Agip Motel,* Circonvallazione Pirri. 57 rooms.

RESTAURANTS: **Italia,* 26 Via Sardegna. ***dal Corsaro,* Viale Regina Margherita 28. ***La Pineta,* Via della Pineta 108.

Capri (pop. 12,300)

HOTELS: (closed Nov. to March unless otherwise indicated) *****Quisisana.* 150 rooms. Luxurious, with gardens and tennis court. Closed January-February. ****Caesar Augustus.* 66 rooms. In Anacapri, on terraced cliff above the sea. ****La Palma,* Via Vittorio Emanuele 39. Air-conditioned. 80 rooms. ****Europa Palace,* 103 rooms. In Anacapri. ***Capri.* 21 rooms. Open all year. ***Nuovo Reale.* 29 rooms. ***Gatto Bianco.* 32 rooms. ***La Floridiana.* 39 rooms. Open all year. *Excelsior Parco,* 30 rooms. ***Tirrenia.* 26 rooms. Swimming pool. ***Villa Margherita.* 26 rooms. A well-run pension. **Florida,* 22 rooms. Open all year.

RESTAURANTS: ****La Canzone del Mare.* Swimming pool and terraces on rocks at Marina Piccola. **Da Gelsomina alla Migliara,* Via Migliara. In Anacapri. In the country. Not accessible by car. Lovely view. ***La Pigna.* Via Lo Palazzo 30. **Sirene,* Via Marina Piccola 63.

Catania (Sicily) (pop. 400,000)

HOTELS: ****Excelsior,* Piazza G. Verga 39. 163 rooms. ****Jolly,* Piazza Trento 13. 159 rooms. **Motel AGIP,* Route 114. 45 rooms. **Plaja.* 42 Viale Kennedy. 45 rooms. **Moderno,* Via Alessi 9. 47 rooms.

RESTAURANTS: ***Pagano al Mare,* 18 Via Acque Casse, Orgnina (4 kms. from Catania).

Como (pop. 99,000)

HOTELS: ***Barchetta Excelsior*, 1 Piazza Cavour. 56 rooms. **Metropole & Suisse*, 19 Piazza Cavour. 70 rooms. **Villa Flori*, Via Prov. per Cernobbio 12. 52 rooms.

RESTAURANTS: ***Cervetta*, 26 Via Cadorna. ***Piazzolo*, Via Indipendenza 65. *Silenzio*, Viale Lecco 25. Specializes in grilled fish.

Cortina d'Ampezzo (pop. 8,600)

HOTELS: ****Miramonti-Majestic*, Via Pezzie 103. 140 rooms. Open December to March; June to September. Tennis courts and golf course. ***Cristallo*, 42 Via R. Menardi. 81 rooms. Open December to March; June to September. Tennis courts and swimming pool. ***Savoia*, 62 Via Roma. 142 rooms. Open December to March; June to September. Swimming pool. **Corona*, 10 Via C. Battisti 15. 46 rooms. Open December to March; June to September. **Europa*, Corso Italia 207. 52 rooms. Closed Nov. to mid-Dec. *Motel AGIP*, 118 Via Roma. 42 rooms.

RESTAURANTS: **Capannina del Boite*, 11 Via Stadio. **Da Beppe Sello*, Via Ronco 68. **Il Meloncino*, On the road to Pocol. In a lovely chalet with a great view.

Elba (Island of) (pop. 27,000)

HOTELS: ***Fabricia* at Magazzini in Porto Ferraio, 70 rooms. Open April to October. ***Hermitage*, Biodola, in Porto Ferraio. Open May to October. 105 rooms. On beach. ***La Primula*, at Marciana Marina. 62 rooms. Open June to October. On beach. ***Del Golfo* at Marciano Procchio. Private beach, pool and tennis. Open all year. 95 rooms.

RESTAURANTS: ***Al Braciere*, Via Carducci 230, in Portoferraio. **La

Ferrigna, Pz della Repubblica, 22. In the old city. Portoferraio.

Ferrara (pop. 147,000)

HOTELS: ***Astra*, 55 Viale Cavour. 82 rooms. **Ripagrande*, Via Ripagrande 21. 42 rooms.

RESTAURANTS: **Italia*, 32 Largo Castello. *La Provvidenza*, 92 Corso Erole D'Este.

Florence (Firenze) (pop. 440,000)

HOTELS: ****Excelsior*, 3 Piazza Ognissanti. 204 rooms. Overlooking the Arno. ***Croce di Malta*, 7 Via della Scala. Heated pool. 98 rooms. ****Savoy*, 7 Piazza della Repubblica. 98 rooms. In center of town. ****Villa Medici*, 42 Via il Prato. 107 rooms. ***Anglo-American*, 9 Via Garibaldi. 116 rooms. ***Continental*, Lungarno Acciaioli 2. In the heart of ancient Florence. 61 rooms. ***Jolly-Carlton*, Piazza Vittorio Veneto 4a. 167 rooms. Swimming pool, air-conditioning. ***Grand Hotel Majestic*, 1 Via del Melarancio. 104 rooms. Near the railroad station. ****Villa La Massa*, Bagno a Ripoli-Candeli, 7 kilometers from Florence. Lovely 18th century palace. Heated pool. 43 rooms. ***Kraft*, 2 Via Solferino. 70 rooms. Air-conditioning, swimming pool and panoramic view. ***Londra*, Via Jacopo da Diacceto 16. 104 rooms. Quiet. ***Minerva Grand Hotel*, Piazza S. Maria Novella. 110 rooms. Pool, garages. ***Plaza Lucchesi*, Lungarno della Zecca Vecchia 38. 105 rooms. On the Arno, air-conditioned. **Lungarno*, Borgo San Jacopo 14. 71 rooms. Air-conditioned. ***Helvetia e Bristol*, Via dei Pescioni 2. 62 rooms. On the river. **Golf*, Viale Tratelli Rosselli 56. 39 rooms. ***Della Signoria*, 1 Via delle Terme. 29 rooms. In center of town. **Pitti Palace* (pension), Via Barbadori 2. 40 rooms.

RESTAURANTS: ***Doney*, 46 Via Tornabuoni. ***Giovacchino*, 2 Via Tosinghi. ***Sabatini Gino*, 9A Via Panzani. **Buca Lapi*, 1 Via del Trebbio. **Buca Mario*, 16R Piazza Ottaviani. *Fagioli*, Corso dei Tintori 47. **13 Gobbi*, 9R Villa della Porcellana. **Paoli*, 12R Via dei Tavolini. *La Fonticine*, Via Nazionale 79R. * Cammillo, 57R Borgo San Jacopo. * Cantinone del Gallo Nero*, Via Santo Spirito, 6/R.

BEST BUYS: *Leather Goods:* Gherardini, 27R Via della Vigna Nuova; Gucci, 73 Via Tornabuoni; Luti, 28R Via di Parione; *Linens and Lingerie:* Testa, Lungarno Guicciardini, 21. *Gi Ba,* Via M. Albertinelli, 10. *Straw goods:* Paoli, 26R Via della Vigna Nuova.

Gardone Riviera (pop. 2,700)

HOTELS: ***Grand*, Via Zanardelli 72. 182 rooms. Garden on the lake. Open April to October. **Astoria*, Barbarano di Salo. 95 rooms. *Villa Capri*, Via Zanardelli 148. 30 rooms.

Genoa (Genova) (pop. 746,700)

HOTELS: ****Colombia*, Via Balbi 40. 172 rooms. Opposite railway stations. ***Savoia Majestic*, 5 Via Arsenale di Terra. 120 rooms. ***Bristol Palace*. 35 Via XX Settembre. 105 rooms. ***Plaza*, 11 Via M. Piaggio. 91 rooms. **City*, Via S. Sebastiano 6. 75 rooms. *Bellevue*, Via Provvidenza 1. 38 rooms. **Londra-Continentale*, 1 Via Arsenale di Terra. 48 rooms.

RESTAURANTS: ***La Santa*, 1 Vico Indoratori. ***Vittorio al Mare*, 1 Belv. E. Firpo, in Boccadasse. **Zeffirino*, Via XX Settembre 20. **Il Cucciolo*, Viale Sauli 33. **Gran Gotto*, Via Fiume 11R.

Ischia (pop. 43,600)

HOTELS: ***Excelsior Belvedere*. 72 rooms. Open May to October. ***

Jolly Hotel Delle Terme, 208 rooms. ***La Reginella*, at Lacco Ameno. 50 rooms. ****Punta Molino Grand Hotel*. 90 rooms. Air-conditioning, swimming pool, private beach. April to October. **Aragona Palace Hotel Terme*, Via Porto 12. 40 rooms.

RESTAURANTS: **Pirozzi* at Ischia Ponte, Via Seminario 53. **San Montano*, at Lido di San Montano. On the beach.

L'Aquila (pop. 66,000)

HOTELS: ***Le Cannelle Hotel Residence*, Borgo Rivera. 142 rooms. * Italia, 79 Corso Vitt. Emanuele. 37 rooms.

RESTAURANT: **Tre Marie*, 3 Via Tre Marie.

La Spezia (pop. 117,000)

HOTELS: ***Jolly*, 2 Via XX Settembre. 110 rooms. *Diana*, 30 Via Colombo. 18 rooms.

RESTAURANT: **Da Carlino*, Pz. Battisti 7.

Leghorn (Livorno) (pop. 176,000)

HOTELS: **Boston*, Pz. Massini 40. 53 rooms. ***Palazzo*, 195 Viale Italia. 125 rooms. **Excelsior*, 1 Via D. Cassuto. 59 rooms. **Giappone*, 65 Via Grande. 56 rooms. **Gennarino*, Viale Italia 301. 23 rooms.

RESTAURANTS: **Giardino Emiliano*, Viale Italia 103. **Antico Moro*, Via Bartelloni, 59.

Mantua (Mantova) (pop. 60,000)

HOTELS: ***San Lorenzo*, Piazza Concordia 14. 44 rooms. **Italia*, 8 Piazza Cavallotti. 30 rooms.

RESTAURANTS: **Il Cigno*, Piazza Carlo d'Arco. Garden. **Ai Garibaldini*, 7 Via San Longino.

Merano (pop. 33,000)

HOTELS: ***Bristol,* 14 Via Ottone Huber. 146 rooms. Open April to October. Swimming pool. ***Savoy,* 1 Via Rezia. 54 rooms. Open April to October. ***Meranerhof,* Via Manzoni 1. 71 rooms. Swimming. ***Palace Kurhotel,* Via Cavour 4. 125 rooms. **Schloss Labers,* Via Labers 25. 32 rooms. Converted medieval castle on hilltop. Swimming.

Milan (Milano) (pop. 1,667,000)

NEAR THE CENTRAL STATION
HOTELS: ****Milano Hilton,* Via Galvani 12. 347 rooms. ****Excelsior Gallia Meridien,* Piazza Duca d'Aosta. 263 rooms. ***Anderson,* Piazza Luigi di Savoia 20. 107 rooms. ***Auriga,* Via Pirelli 7. 64 rooms. ***Royal,* Via Cardano 1. 110 rooms. ***Splendido,* Via Andrea Doria 4. 156 rooms. **Augustus,* Via Napo Torriani 29. 56 rooms.

RESTAURANTS: ***Cavallini,* Via Mauro Macchi 2. **Al Griso,* Via Fabio Filzi 12.

CENTER OF THE CITY
HOTELS: ***Select,* Via Baracchini 12, 140 rooms. ****Grand Hotel et de Milan,* Via Manzoni 29. 90 rooms. ***Dei Cavalieri,* Piazza Missori 1. 177 rooms. ****Grand Hotel Duomo,* Via San Raffaele 1. 158 rooms. ***Carlton Senato,* Via Senato 5. 78 rooms. ***Cavour,* Via Fatebenefratelli 21. 113 rooms. ***De La Ville,* Via Hoepli 6. 105 rooms. ****Jolly President,* Largo Augusto. 230 rooms. ***Plaza,* Piazza Diaz 3. 120 rooms. **Ambasciatori.* Galleria del Corso 3. 92 rooms.

RESTAURANTS: ***Alfio Cavour,* Via Senato 31. ***Savini,* Via Ugo Foscolo 5 (Galleria Vitt. Emanuele). *** St. Andrews, via Sant'Andrea 23. *** Biffi Scala,* Piazza della Scala 1.

***San Maurilio,* Via S. Maurilio 17. ***L'Assassino,* Via Amedei 8. **Don Lisander,* Via Manzoni 12.

NORTHEAST
HOTELS: ****Palace,* Piazza della Repubblica 20. 182 rooms. ****Principe di Savoia,* Piazza della Repubblica 17. 285 rooms. ***Manin,* Via Manin 7. 110 rooms. ***Jolly Touring,* Via Tarchetti 2. 270 rooms. *** Windsor, Via Galileo Galilei 2. 114 rooms.

RESTAURANTS: ***Riccione,* Via Taramelli 70. ***Cassina de' Pomm,* Via M. Gioia 194. ***Da Lino,* Via Casati 12. **Montecristo,* Corso Sempione and Via Prina 17. *** Taverna del Gran Sasso, Piazza Principessa Clotilde 10. ***Abbadesse,* Via Abbadesse 20. **La Secchia Rapita,* Viale Marche 56.

NORTHWEST
HOTELS: ***Capitol,* Via Cimarosa 6. 100 rooms.

RESTAURANTS: ***Romani,* Via Trebazio 3. ***Grattacielo,* Via Vittor Pisani 6. **Tre Pini,* Via Tullo Morgagni 19. ***Da Gigi il Cacciatore,* Via Procaccini 54. **Da Fumino,* Via Bernina 43. *A Riccione,* Via Taramelli, 70. **Gran San Bernardo,* Via Borgese 14. **Serafino,* Via Bramante 35.

SOUTHEAST
HOTELS: **D'Este,* Viale Bligny 23. 54 rooms.

RESTAURANTS: ***Giannino,* Via A. Sciesa 8. ***Vecchia Milano,* Via Gian Galeazzo 25. ***Scaletta,* Pzle. Stazione Genoa. **Al Porto,* Pzle. Generale Cantore. **Sciué Sciué,* Via Solari, 6. **Da Giordano,* Via Torti.

SOUTHWEST
HOTELS: *Motel dei Fiori,* Via La Spezia.

RESTAURANTS: ***La Corba, Via Dei Gigli 14. *La Cantinetta, Via Ripamonti, 19.

Naples (Napoli) (pop. 1,224,000)

HOTELS: ****Excelsior, 48 Via Partenope. 136 rooms. On the waterfront. ***Vesuvio, 45 Via Partenope. 178 rooms. Busy and popular. ***Jolly Ambassador's, 70 Via Medina. 251 rooms. ***Santa Lucia, Via Partenope 46. 132 rooms. ***Parker's, 135 Corso Vittorio Emanuele. 87 rooms. ***Royal, 38 Via Partenope. 316 rooms. **Paradiso, Via Catullo 11. 74 rooms.

RESTAURANTS: **Transatlantico, Via Malpighi 3, a wharfside restaurant with both excellent food and atmosphere. Pizzeria Bellini, Via S. Maria Costantinopoli, 80. **Da Ciro a Santa Brigida, 71 Via Santa Brigida. *Ettore, Via S. Lucia, 56. **Cinquantatre, Pz. Dante, 53.

Orvieto (pop. 23,000)

HOTELS: ***Grand Hotel Italia, Piazza del Popolo 13. 40 rooms. *** La Badia, La Badia. 22 rooms.

RESTAURANTS: **Morino, 37 Via Garibaldi. **Del Pino da Checco, 14 Via di Piazza del Popolo.

Padua (Padova) (pop. 234,000)

HOTELS: ***Plaza, Corso Milano 40. 142 rooms. **Monaco, Piazzale Stazione 3. 54 rooms. **Europa Zaramella, Largo Europa 9. 57 rooms.

RESTAURANTS: ***Isola di Caprera, Via Marsillio da Padova 5. **Dotto, Via Squarcione 23.

Palermo (Sicily) (pop. 712,000)

HOTELS: ****Villa Igiea, Salita Belmonte. 120 rooms. Stunning garden and view of Gulf of Palermo. *** Grand Hotel et des Palmes, 398 Via

Roma. 187 rooms. ***Jolly, 22 Foro Italico. 290 rooms. **Ponte, Via Crispi 99. 137 rooms. **Sole, 291 Corso Vittorio Emanuele. 180 rooms.

RESTAURANTS: Pedro al Ficodindia, Via E. Amari 64, near the port. *Le Caprice, 42 Via Cavour.

Parma (pop. 175,000)

HOTELS: ***Park Stendhal, 3 Piazza Bodoni. 60 rooms. ***Palace Hotel Maria Luigia, Viale Mentana 140. 105 rooms. **Enrico I, Via. G.B. Borghesi 12. 15 rooms. **Button, Borgo Salina 7. 42 rooms. *Moderno, 4 Via Cecchi. 47 rooms.

RESTAURANTS: **Aurora, Volta Sant'Alessandro 4. **Cocchi, Via Gramsci 16.

Perugia (pop. 144,000)

HOTELS: ****Brufani Palace, 12 Piazza Italia. 24 rooms. **La Rosetta, 19 Piazza Italia. 96 rooms.

RESTAURANTS: **La Taverna, Via delle Streghe 8. **Del Sole, Via della Rupe 1. *Falchetto, Via Bartolo 20.

Pisa (pop. 103,000)

HOTELS: ***Cavalieri, Piazza della Stazione. 102 rooms. ***Grand Hotel Duomo, 94 Via Santa Maria. 90 rooms. **Arno, Piazza della Repubblica 6. 30 rooms. **La Pace, 14 Via Gramsci. 72 rooms.

RESTAURANTS: **Buzzino, 44 Via Cammeo. *Nando, 8 Via Contessa Matilde.

Portofino (pop. 710)

HOTELS: ****Splendido. Salita Baratta 13. 77 rooms. March to December. **Nazionale. 40 rooms. ** Piccolo Hotel. 27 rooms.

RESTAURANT: **Miramare, Calata Doria 66.

Positano (pop. 3,100)

HOTELS: ****Le Sirenuse.* Via C. Colombo 30. 62 rooms. Open all year. ***Miramare,* Via Trara Genoino 30. 18 rooms. April to October. **Buca di Bacco,* Via Rampa Teglia 8. 53 rooms. **Royal,* Via Pasitea. 69 rooms.

RESTAURANT: **Buca di Bacco.*

Rapallo (pop. 27,000)

HOTELS: ****Grand Hotel Bristol,* Via Aurelia Orientale 369. 93 rooms. ***Eurotel Rapallo,* Via Aurelia Ponente 22. 67 rooms. Pool, air-conditioned. **Savoia,* 1 Piazza IV Novembre 3. 50 rooms. **Moderne & Royal,* 6 Via Gramsci. 48 rooms.

RESTAURANTS: **Elite,* Via Milite Ignoto 19. **Nicola,* 79 Via Mamelli.

Ravello (pop. 2,400)

HOTELS: **Rufolo,* Via S. Francesco. 28 rooms. Swimming pool. **Caruso Belvedere,* Via Toro 52. 27 rooms.

Ravenna (pop. 136,000)

HOTELS: ***Jolly,* 1 Piazza Mameli. 80 rooms. ***Park Hotel Ravenna,* Viale delle Nazioni 181, Marina di Ravenna. Open April to Dec. 146 rooms.

RESTAURANTS: **Alle Torre,* Via Paolo Costa 3. *Scai,* Piazza Baracca.

Rimini (pop. 129,000)

HOTELS: ****Grand Hotel,* Piazzale Indipendenza, 150 rooms. Pool, tennis, beach. **Sporting,* Viale Vespucci 20, at the Lido. 78 rooms. May to Sept. ***Ambasciatori,* Viale A. Vespucci 22. 66 rooms. ***Residenza Grand Hotel,* Piazzale Indipendenza. 50 rooms. **Napoleon,* Piazza C. Battisti 22. 64 rooms. **Sporting,* Viale Amerigo Vespucci 20. 78 rooms.

RESTAURANTS: **Belvedere,* Molo di Levante. At the port. **Vecchia Rimini,* 33 Via Cattaneo.

Rome (Roma) (pop. 2,840,000)

HOTELS:

Via Veneto-Piazza Barberini section ****Palazzo Ambasciatori,* 70 Via Vittorio Veneto. 150 rooms. ****Bernini-Bristol,* 23 Piazza Barberini. 124 rooms. ****Eden,* 49 Via Ludovisi. 117 rooms. ****Excelsior,* 125 Via Vittorio Veneto. 367 rooms. ***Flora,* 191 Via Vittorio Veneto. 185 rooms. ***Eliseo,* 30 Via di Porta Pinciana. 52 rooms. ***Regina Carlton.* 72 Via Vittorio Veneto. 134 rooms. ***Savoy,* 15 Via Ludovisi. 110 rooms. ***Victoria,* 41 Via Campania. 110 rooms. **Elite,* Via Francesco Crispi 49. 25 rooms. *Tefi,* Via San Basilio 53. 13 rooms. **Villa del Parco,* Via Nomentana 110. 23 rooms. *Dinesen,* 18 Via di Porta Pinciana. 32 rooms.

Piazza di Spagna-Trinita de' Monti section
****De la Ville,* 67 Via Sistina. 197 rooms. ***Marini Strand,* 17 Via del Tritone. 118 rooms. ***Internazionale,* 79 Via Sistina. 38 rooms.

Railroad Terminal section
****Le Grand,* 3 Via Vittorio Emanuele Orlando. 171 rooms. ****Parco dei Principi,* Via G. Frescobaldi 5. 203 rooms. ***Commodore,* Via Torino 1. 65 rooms. Air-conditioned. ***Royal Santina,* Via Marsala 22. 121 rooms. Air-conditioned. ***Universo,* Via Principe Amedeo 5. 226 rooms. Air-conditioned. ****Forum,* Via Tor de' Conti 25–30. 90 rooms. Overlooking ruins of the Forum of Augustus. ***Massimo d'Azeglio,* 18 Via Cavour. 209 rooms. ***Metropole,* 3 Via Principe Amedeo. 285 rooms. ***Palatino,* Via Cavour 213. 202 rooms. ***San Giorgio,* 61 Via G. Amendola.

186 rooms. **Nord-Nuovo Roma*, 3 Via G. Amendola. 150 rooms.

Other sections

****Cavalieri Hilton*, Via Cadlolo 101, on Monte Mario. 387 rooms. The poshest hotel in town. ***Villa Pamphili*, Via della Noccetta, 105. Near the Pamphili Park. 257 rooms. ***Dei Congressi*, 29 Viale Shakespeare. 97 rooms. In EUR exposition section. ***Michelangelo*, 14 Via Stazione di S. Pietro. Near St. Peter's. 150 rooms. ***Cardinal*, Via Giulia 62. 66 rooms. ***Plaza*, 126 Via del Corso. 207 rooms. In shopping district. ***Colonna Palace*, Piazza Montecitorio 12. 110 rooms. ***Raphael*, 2 Largo Febo. 100 rooms. Behind Piazza Navona. **Columbus*, 33 Via della Conciliazione. 123 rooms. Near St. Peter's. **Claridge*, Via Liegi, 62. In Parioli. 88 rooms. *Motel Salaria*, Via Salaria, 256. Quite near the city. 29 rooms.

RESTAURANTS: ***Alfredo All-'Augusteo*, 30 Piazza Augusto Imperatore. ***Alfredo alla Scrofa*, 104 Via della Scrofa. ***El Toulà*, Via della Lupa 29, Venetian specialties. ***Casina Valadier*, in Villa Borghese. View of city from terrace. ***George's*, 7 Via Marche. International cuisine. ***Hostaria dell'Orso*, 93 Via Monte Brianzo. 15th-century palazzo turned into restaurant and nightclub. Dancing. ***Il Casale*, Via Flaminia, 10 kilometers from Rome. Sprawling old farmhouse featuring superb *antipasti*. ***Passetto*, 14 Via Zanardelli. ***Ranieri*, 26 Via Mario dei Fiori. Old-fashioned, dignified, quiet. **al Chianti*, 17–19 Via Ancona. Specializes in game dishes. **Taverna Flavia*, 9 Via Flavia. Long a favorite of Roman aristocracy. **Corsetti*, 27 Piazza San Cosimato. Sea food specialties. **Dal Bolognese*, Piazza del Popolo. Bolognese specialties. Summer terrace. **Ernesto alla Cassia*, 59

Via Oriolo Romano, just out of town. Branch of city restaurant for outdoor country dining. **Fontanella*, Largo Fontanella di Borghese 86. Florentine specialties, game and steaks. **Galeassi*, Piazza Santa Maria in Trastevere. Summer terrace on picturesque piazza. **Il Buco*, 8 Via Sant'Ignazio. Florentine specialties. **Al Moro*, 13 Vicolo delle Bollette. Near the Trevi Fountain. **Otello*, 81 Via della Croce. Outdoor dining in courtyard. **Nino*, 11 Via Borgognona. Florentine specialties. **Al Vero Amatriciano*, Via Rasella 130. A typical Roman kitchen. **Piccolo Mondo*, 39/d Via Aurora. Crowded and friendly. **da Mario*, 55 Via della Vite. One of Rome's best small *trattorias*. **Carmelo alla Rosetta*, 9 Via della Rosetta. Seafood specialties. **Cecilia Metella*, 125 Via Appia Antica. Summer terrace on old Appian Way. **Tre Scalini*, 30 Piazza Navona. Terrace on famous piazza. **Ulpia*, 2 Piazza Foro Traiano. Ancient Roman atmosphere. *Lucia*, Vic.lo. del Mattonato, 79. In Trastevere. *Angelino*, 37 Piazza Margana. Outdoor dining on charming piazza. *Checco & Carrettiere*, 10 Via Benedetta. Trastevere atmosphere. *Giggetto*, 21 a Via Portico d'Ottavia. Unpretentious, old Rome atmosphere in heart of former ghetto. **Papa Giovanni*, 4 Via dei Sediari (off Piazza Navona). Small, intimate, truffle dishes a specialty.

BEST BUYS: *Leather goods:* Gucci, 8 Via Condotti; Ceresa & Rampone, 118 Via Tritone (less expensive branch at 90 Via Tritone); Navarro, Piazza Mignanelli 22. *Gloves:* Catello D'Auria, Via Due Macelli 55; Selú Guanti, Via Cavour 39; Ugucas, Via del Tritone 145; D'Auria, Via Due Macelli 55; Perrone, 92 Piazza di Spagna; *Men's ties, sweaters, accessories;* Cucci, 67 Via Condotti; Avenia, Via del Corso 164; Battistoni, 61 Via

Condotti; Ibbas, 50 Via Condotti. *Decorative glassware:* Venini, 61A Via Condotti; Navarrini, Via del Corso 507. *Silk fabrics:* Aston, Via Piemonte 42; Galtrucco, 18 Via Tritone; Polidori, 4c Via Borgognona. *Linens:* Cesari, Via Barbarini 1; Bellini, 77 Piazza di Spagna; II Merletto, 301 Via del Corso. *Gifts:* Myricae, 36 Via Frattina; *De Simone Ceramiche,* Via Margutta 47/A. *Antiques:* Stores along Via del Babuino and Via dei Coronari.

San Marino (Republic of) (pop. 18,-300)

HOTELS: ***Grand Hotel San Marino,* Viale Antonio Omofri 31. 55 rooms. **Excelsior,* Via Jacopo Istriani. 26 rooms. ***Titano,* Contrada del Collegio 21. 50 rooms. **Titanino,* Via Giovanni di Simone delle Penne. 12 rooms.

RESTAURANTS: ***Da Alfio,* Via del Serrone. **Nido del Falco,* Salita alla Roccas. Open April to September.

San Martino Di Castrozza (pop. 300)

HOTELS: ***Savoia,* Via Passo Rolle 233. 72 rooms. **Delle Nazioni.* 38 rooms. Open all year.

San Remo (pop. 62,000)

HOTELS: ****Royal,* 80 Corso Imperatrice. 139 rooms. Closed Oct.-Nov. Swimming pool. ***Mediterranee,* 76 Corso Cavallotti, 62 rooms. ****Astoria West End,* 8 Corso Matuzia. 110 rooms. ****Londra,* 2 Corso Matuzia. 160 rooms. Open Dec. to Oct. **** Miramare Continental Palace,* 9 Corso Matuzia. 68 rooms. Closed October and November. ***Europa & della Pace,* 27 Corso Imperatrice. 78 rooms.

RESTAURANTS: ****Au Rendez-Vous,* 126 Via Matteotti. ***Gambero Rosso,* 71 Corso Matteotti. ***Pesce d'Oro,* 270 Corso Cavallotti.

Santa Margherita Ligure (pop. 21,-600)

HOTELS: *****Imperial Palace,* 19 Via Pagana. 106 rooms. Closed Nov. and Dec. ****Miramare,* 30 Via Milite Ignoto. Open December to October. 81 rooms. ****Park Hotel Suisse,* 31 Via Favale. Swimming pool. 85 rooms. Open May to October. ****Continental,* 8 Via Pagana. 76 rooms.

RESTAURANTS: ***Brace,* 43 Sal. Montebello. ***La Ghiaia,* 5 Via Andrea Doria. **Bassa Prora,* 7 Via Garibaldi.

Sestriere (pop. 800)

HOTELS: ****Grand Hotel Sestriere.* 93 rooms. ****Cristallo,* Via Pinerolo 5. 72 rooms.

Siena (pop. 66,000)

HOTELS: ****Villa Scacciapensieri,* 24 Via di Scacciapensieri. 35 rooms. Just outside city. Open March to October. ***Palazzo Ravizza,* 34 Pian dei Mantellini. 28 rooms. A well-run pension.

RESTAURANTS: ***Alla Speranza,* Piazza del Campo. ***Guido,* 7 Vicolo Pettinaio. **Tullio-Tre Cristi,* 1 Vicolo Provenzano.

Sorrento (pop. 17,600)

HOTELS: ****Grand Hotel Vesuvio,* Via Nastro Verde 7. 190 rooms. **** Excelsior Grand Vittoria.* Piazza Torquato Tasso 34. 122 rooms. ****Cesare Augusto,* Viale degli Aranci. 120 rooms. Pool. ****Riviera,* Via Califano 22. 91 rooms. Pool. ****Carlton.* Via Correale 15. 70 rooms.

RESTAURANTS: **La Minervetta,* 25 Via Capo. Terrace with sea view. **La Tonnarella,* 31 Via Capo. Sea view.

Stresa (pop. 5,200)

HOTELS: *****Grand Hotel et des Iles Borromées,* 67 Corso Umberto I. 168

rooms. One of Italy's most famous hotels. Open all year. ***Regina Palace, Corso Umberto I 27. 176 rooms. Open April to October. ***Bristol, Lungolago Umberto I. 250 rooms. Open March to October. ***Astoria, 31 Lungolago Umberto I. 98 rooms. Open March to October. **La Perla Nera Lido Hotel, Viale Lido 25. 27 rooms. **La Palma, Lungolago Umberto 1. 128 rooms. On the lake, swimming.

RESTAURANTS: *Luina, 21 Via Garibaldi. **Del Pescatore, Vicolo del Poncivo 3.

Syracuse (Siracusa), Sicily, (pop. 116,000)

HOTELS: ***Jolly, Corso Gelone 45. 102 rooms. **Park Hotel, Via Filisto 80. 99 rooms.

RESTAURANT: *Darsena, 4 Riva Garibaldi.

Taormina (Sicily) (pop. 10,200)

HOTELS: ****San Domenico, 5 Piazza San Domenico. 117 rooms. 16th-century monastery turned into luxury hotel. Fabulous view, extensive garden, and excellent food—by far the best in town.

Taranto (pop. 247,000)

HOTELS: ***Delfino, 66 Viale Virgilio. 198 rooms. **Plaza, Via D'Aquino 46, 112 rooms. Air-conditioned.

RESTAURANTS: **L'Assassino, 29 Via Lungomare Vittorio Emanuele III. ***Al Gambero, 4 Via Vico del Ponte.

Trento (pop. 99,000)

HOTELS: ***Trento, Via Alfieri 3. 94 rooms.

RESTAURANTS: **Roma, Via S. Simonino. **Le Bollicine, 1 Via dei Ventuno at the Castello del Buonconsiglio. Refined atmosphere. *Birreria Forst, Via Oss Mazurana 38.

Trieste (pop. 260,000)

HOTELS: ***Grand Hotel Duchi d'Aosta, 2 Piazzale Unità d'Italia. 52 rooms. ***Savoia Excelsior Palace, 4 Riva Mandracchio. 154 rooms. ***Jolly, 7 Corso Cavour. 177 rooms. **Corso, 2 Via San Spiridione. 82 rooms. *Roma, 7 Via C. Ghega. 38 rooms.

RESTAURANTS: **Al Granzo, Piazza Venezia 7. ***Antica Suban, 2 Via Comici. Pleasant summer garden. **Bottega del Vino, Piazzale Milizie 3. Inside Castello San Giusto.

Turin (Torino) (pop. 1,172,000)

HOTELS: ***Jolly Principi di Piemonte, 15 Via P. Gobetti. 109 rooms. ***Jolly Ambasciatori, 104 Corso Vittorio Emanuele. 200 rooms. ***Jolly Ligure, Piazza Carlo Felice 85. 180 rooms. ***Concord, 47 Via Lagrange. 139 rooms. ***Sitea, 35 Via Carlo Alberto. 120 rooms. ***Palace Hotel Turin, 8 Via Sacchi. 125 rooms. ***Majestic, Corso V. Emanuele 54. 159 rooms. **Alexandra, Lungo Dora Napoli 14. 50 rooms. **Luxor, Corso Stati Uniti 7. 63 rooms.

RESTAURANTS: ***Gatto Nero, 14 Corso Filippo Turati. ***San Giorgio, in Parco Valentino (the old section of the city), overlooking the Po. Dancing. **Tre Galline, 37 Via Bellezia. Fondue and other regional dishes. ***Cambio, 2 Piazza Carignano. Old, dignified. ***Villa Sassi, 47 Str. Traforo Pino. 18th-century park in hills, 4 kms. from city. **Fortin, 8 Via Chiesa. **Due Lampioni, 45 Via Carlo Alberto. *Giappone, 16 Via Galliari.

Venice (Venezia) (pop. 355,000)

HOTELS: ****Bauer Gruenwald, S. Marco 1459. 210 rooms. ****Danieli

Royal Excelsior, Riva degli Schiavoni 4191. 238 rooms. ****Europa e Regina,* 2159 San Marco. 199 rooms. ****Gritti Palace,* Campo Santa Maria del Giglio 2467. 90 rooms. ****Cipriani,* 10 Giudecca. 94 rooms. Open April-Oct. ****Gabrielli-Sandwirth,* Riva degli Schiavoni 4. 110 rooms. ***Londra Palace,* Riva degli Schiavoni 4171. 67 rooms. ***Luna,* 1243 San Marco-Ascensione. 122 rooms. ***Monaco & Grand Canal,* 1325 San Marco. 75 rooms. ***ETAP Park Hotel,* Giardino Papadopoli. 100 rooms. ***Metropole,* 4149 Riva degli Schiavoni. 65 rooms. **Bonvecchiati,* 4488 San Marco. 86 rooms. **Boston,* 848 San Marco. Calle dei Fabbri. 46 rooms. ***Cavalletto & Doge Orseolo,* 1107 San Marco. 87 rooms. **Casanova,* 1284 San Marco. 45 rooms. ** *La Fenice et des Artistes,* 1936 San Marco. 64 rooms.

At the Lido of Venice ****Excelsior Palace,* 41 Lungomare Marconi. 230 rooms. Open April to October. ****Des Bains,* 17 Lungomare Marconi. 247 rooms. Open May to September. ***Quattro Fontane,* 16 Via Quattro Fontane. 72 rooms. Open all year. **Helvetia,* Gran Viale 4-6. 60 rooms.

RESTAURANTS: ***Antico Martini,* Campo San Fantin 1983. International cuisine. Open April-October. ***La Fenice,* 1937 San Marco. *** *Harry's Bar,* Calle Vallaresso 1323. A landmark. ***Do Forni,* Calle dei Specchieri 468. ***La Caravella,* Calle Larga 22 Marzo. ***Peoceto Risorto,* Rialto San Polo 249. **

Colomba, Piscina de Frezzeria 1665. Extensive collection of contemporary paintings. **Noemi,* Calle dei fabbri 99. *Ridotto Grill,* 1337 San Marco.

BEST BUYS: *Decorative glassware:* Salviati, 195 San Gregorio and 79 Piazza San Marco; Venini, 314 Piazzetta Leoncini and Island of Murano. *Lace:* Olga Asta, 128 Piazza San Marco and Island of Burano.

Verona (pop. 269,000)

HOTELS: ****Due Torri,* 4 Piazza S. Anastasia. 100 rooms. ***Colomba d'Oro,* 10 Via C. Cattaneo. 56 rooms. ***Grand,* 105 Corso Porta Nuova. 55 rooms. ***Accademia,* 12 Via Scala. 116 rooms. **Victoria,* Via Adua 8. 42 rooms.

RESTAURANTS: **Dodici Apostoli,* 3 Corticella San Marco. **Poste Vece,* 1608 S. Polo. Near the fish market. ***Tre Corone,* 16 Piazza Brà *Al Bragozzo,* 13 Via del Pontiere. *Torcolo "Da Pomari,"* 11 Via Carlo Cattaneo.

Vicenza (pop. 118,000)

HOTELS: **Continental,* Via Trissino. 50 rooms. **Motelagip,* Via Scaligeri 68. 66 rooms. New, air-conditioned. **Cristina,* 32 Corso San Felice. 24 rooms. **City,* Viale Verona 12. 23 rooms. ***Jolly,* 27 Viale Roma. 35 rooms.

RESTAURANTS: *Vecchia Guardia,* 15 Via Pescherie Vecchie, Near Pz. dei Signori. **Pedavena,* 93 Viale Verona. **Al Pozzo,* Via Sant'Antonio 1.

INDEX